The Post-16 SENCO Handbook

This accessible, practical handbook provides essential guidance to SENCOs in sixth forms and colleges of further education on how to manage the support of students with additional needs, and how to work with their colleagues, students' families and external professionals to co-ordinate effective provision. As a result of the revised Code of Practice 0–25 years (2015) it has been necessary for the FE sector to develop a new approach to the responsibility for, and support of, students with learning difficulties and disabilities.

With up-to-date information on supporting and taking responsibility for learners with SEN and disabilities, this book offers practical advice and guidance on:

- The expectations of Further Education colleges and an overview of the learning difficulties/disabilities that they may need to support;
- assessment methods and the importance of consistent, ongoing vigilance and analysis;
- the roles, responsibilities and staff specialism involved in providing different support for different needs;
- requesting and reviewing Education, Health and Care Plans;
- working with families, carers, schools and other external professionals;
- planning for the onward transition of a learner's further education experience.

The Post-16 SENCO Handbook will be essential reading for those involved with provision for post-16 students with additional learning needs who want to deepen their knowledge and enhance their practice.

Elizabeth Ramshaw, MEd, EdD is an experienced practitioner in the field of special education, particularly in the context of post-16 settings. She has been teaching and training governors and teachers for over 20 years and, most recently has also been teaching on the National Award for SEN Co-ordination course in the UK.

nasen
Helping Everyone Achieve

nasen is a professional membership association that supports all those who work with or care for children and young people with special and additional educational needs. Members include teachers, teaching assistants, support workers, other educationalists, students and parents.

nasen supports its members through policy documents, journals, its magazine *Special*, publications, professional development courses, regional networks and newsletters. Its website contains more current information such as responses to government consultations. **nasen's** published documents are held in very high regard both in the UK and internationally.

Other titles published in association with the National Association for Special Educational Needs (nasen):

Understanding and Supporting Pupils with Moderate Learning Difficulties in the Secondary School: A practical guide
Rachael Hayes and Pippa Whittaker
2016/pb: 978-1-138-01910-2

Assessing Children with Specific Learning Difficulties: A teacher's practical guide
Gavin Reid, Gad Elbeheri and John Everatt
2016/pb: 978-0-415-67027-2

Supporting Children with Down's Syndrome, 2ed
Lisa Bentley, Ruth Dance, Elizabeth Morling, Susan Miller and Susan Wong
2016/pb: 978-1-138-91485-8

Provision Mapping and the SEND Code of Practice: Making it work in primary, secondary and special schools, 2ed
Anne Massey
2016/pb: 978-1-138-90707-2

Supporting Children with Medical Conditions, 2ed
Susan Coulter, Lesley Kynman, Elizabeth Morling, Francesca Murray, Jill Wing and Rob Grayson
2016/pb: 978-1-138-91491-9

Achieving Outstanding Classroom Support in Your Secondary School: Tried and tested strategies for teachers and SENCOs
Jill Morgan, Cheryl Jones and Sioned Booth-Coates
2016/pb: 978-1-138-83373-9

Supporting Children with Sensory Impairment
Gill Blairmires, Cath Coupland, Tracey Galbraith, Elizabeth Morling, Jon Parker, Annette Parr, Fiona Simpson and Paul Thornton
2016/pb: 978-1-138-91919-8

The SENCO Survial Guide, 2ed
Sylvia Edwards
2016/pb: 978-1-138-93126-8

Dyslexia and Early Childhood
Barbara Pavey
2016/pb 978-0-415-73652-7

Supporting Children with Dyslexia, 2ed
Hilary Bohl and Sue Hoult
2016/pb 978-1-138-18561-6

More Trouble with Maths: A teacher's complete guide to identifying and diagnosing mathematical difficulties, 2ed
Steve Chinn
2016/pb 978-1-138-18750-4

Supporting Children with Cerebral Palsy, 2ed
Rob Grayson, Jillian Wing, Hannah Tusiine, Graeme Oxtoby and Elizabeth Morling
2017/pb 978-1-138-18742-9

Supporting Children with Behaviour Issues in the Classroom, 2ed
Sarah Carr, Susan Coulter, Elizabeth Morling and Hannah Smith
2017/pb 978-1-138-67385-4

The Post-16 SENCO Handbook

An Essential Guide to Policy and Practice

Elizabeth Ramshaw

Routledge
Taylor & Francis Group
LONDON AND NEW YORK

nasen
Helping Everyone Achieve

First published 2017
by Routledge
2 Park Square, Milton Park, Abingdon, Oxon OX14 4RN

and by Routledge
711 Third Avenue, New York, NY 10017

Routledge is an imprint of the Taylor & Francis Group, an informa business

British Library Cataloguing in Publication Data
A catalogue record for this book is available from the British Library

Library of Congress Cataloging in Publication Data
A catalog record for this book has been requested

ISBN: 978-1-138-65464-8 (hbk)
ISBN: 978-1-138-65465-5 (pbk)
ISBN: 978-1-315-62311-5 (ebk)

Typeset in Galliard
by Saxon Graphics Ltd, Derby

Contents

Illustrations

Tables

Figures

Abbreviations

ADD	Attention deficit disorder
ADHD	Attention deficit hyperactivity disorder
AS	Asperger syndrome
ASD	Autistic spectrum disorder
BDA	British Dyslexia Association
Cert Ed	Certificate in Education
CPD	Continuing professional development
DfE	Department for Education
EFA	Education Funding Agency
EHCP	Education Health Care Plan
EP	Educational psychologist
FE	Further education
GB	Governing body
HI	Hearing impairment
HLTA	Higher Level Teaching Assistant
IEP	Individual Education Plan
ILP	Individual Learning Plan
ILR	Individual Learner Record
LA	Local authority
LSW	Learning Support Worker
MLD	Moderate learning difficulties
MSI	Multi-sensory impairment
PCA	Personal Care Assistant
PGCE	Postgraduate Certificate in Education
QTLS	Qualified Teacher Learning and Skills
SENCO	Special Educational Needs Co-ordinator
SEND	Special educational needs and disabilities
SFA	Skills Funding Agency
SLD	Severe learning difficulty
SMT	Senior management team
SP	Student Profile
SpLD	Specific Learning Difficulty
TA	Teaching Assistant
VI	Visual impairment

Acknowledgements

My thanks are due to the many further education SENCOs, from a vast range of different settings throughout the country, who have contributed their various experiences during the preparation of this book. Similarly, I am grateful to the personnel from rural, urban, large, small, county and unitary local authorities who have informed the background. All their comments, together with those of students studying on the National Award for Special Educational Needs Co-ordinators at the University of Gloucestershire, have proved invaluable regarding the focus of the different chapters.

I would like to thank Alison Foyle, Sarah Tuckwell and Sarah Richardson for their patience, support and guidance throughout the journey of the book.

Finally, my thanks go to Joe Baldwin for his time and support, his enthusiasm for the project, his willingness to serve as my sounding board and for his constructive feedback.

Introduction

> There is no legal duty on colleges to have a SENCO, but colleges should ensure there is a named person in the college with an oversight of SEN provision to ensure co-ordination of support.
>
> (Department for Education (DfE), 2014)

A SENCO by any other name!

The aim of this book is to provide advice and guidance to those working in the further education (FE) sector who have a particular responsibility for the provision of support for young people with learning difficulties and/or disabilities. It is not suggested that this is a new concept; indeed support has been provided in a variety of ways and to a range of different standards over many years. However, recent legislation requires that colleges should embrace the systems and procedures which have applied to schools for some time and which previously ceased as young people reached the age of 16. The SEND Code of Practice 0–25 years 2014 (revised 2015) has meant that schools have been required to revise their systems of administration. For the FE sector, however, a whole new range of ways of recording and collaborating is needed and, additionally in many cases, a new approach to the responsibility for, and support of, students with learning difficulties/disabilities.

It is intended that this book will offer practical guidance to professionals in FE to help them to meet the legal requirements in the most efficient manner, work collaboratively with their colleagues across their setting and beyond and, most importantly, ensure the best possible provision for students who require additional support of any kind.

It is a relatively recent development that the Code of Practice[1] extends its range to cover young people up to the age of 25 and, for this reason, it is timely that those working with young adults from the age of 16 to the age of 25 should receive the guidance not previously required. Primary and secondary schools have, for many years, been familiar with the legislative requirements of Codes of Practice in respect of pupils with additional needs and have developed systems to meet these. Some post-16 settings attached to secondary schools, therefore, may have access to systems already in place to meet the extended age range of the revised Code. For others, however, the requirements may be new and appear daunting. The intention of this book is to guide the latter group with practical advice and signposts to further sources of support.

The provision of education for learners between the ages of 16 and 25 is designed in numerous ways. The Department for Education's (DfE) guidance (2014) for those working in the post-16 sector illustrates the range of ways in which FE provision may be delivered. Sixth form centres, for instance, may be attached to secondary schools. FE colleges may offer vocational and/or academic courses only, while other colleges also accommodate a discrete provision for a Life Skills/Foundation Tier and other students with learning difficulties and/or disabilities. Some providers cater solely for this latter group. This list is not exhaustive but seeks to describe the varied models of provision for post-16 learners.

What's in a name?

Just as post-16 educational provision varies, so does the nomenclature referring to the person responsible for co-ordinating aspects of it that relate to learning support. In some settings, the term SENCO or SENDCO is used, reflecting the terms used in most schools. In other settings Learning Support Co-ordinator/Learning Support Manager may be used. In the interests of brevity, the term SENCO will be used throughout this book. Those of you who hold similar positions but have different titles, please 'translate' this term for your own purpose and do not be offended if it does not exactly match your own title!

Aspects of provision covered in this book are:

- the background and context of the provision for young people with learning difficulties and disabilities;
- the requirements of the SEND Code of Practice 0–25 years;
- the context and role of the SENCO;
- assessment, identification and planning;
- identifying, managing and budgeting for support needs;
- working with colleagues, including senior management, to ensure appropriate and effective provision;
- administration and procedures;
- working with families, schools, local authorities (LAs) and other professionals;
- planning for transition, both into and out of FE.

Of course, the management of these aspects will vary in accordance with the context of the education provider. As described previously, there are numerous ways in which provision can be designed. As each topic is examined, where appropriate, references and guidance will be offered to cover different patterns of provision. In this way, the reader can focus on the support which relates to their own particular setting and their role within it.

It is hoped that, whatever the make-up of the context in which individual SENCOs work, this Handbook will offer guidance and increase their confidence when undertaking the important role of supporting their vulnerable young charges.

Note

1 The term 'Code of Practice' refers to the SEND Code of Practice 0–25 years, unless otherwise stated.

Table I.1 Designs of post-16 provision

Sixth form Sixth-form centre 16–19 academy	These settings, if attached to a secondary school, will already draw on the experience of the school, which will have been working with successive Codes of Practice for many years. It is likely therefore that existing practices may be extended post-16 and that expertise already in place may be shared.
FE college offering mainstream courses – specialist, vocational, academic	This is the setting in which, potentially, the most change will be required with regard to the provision of support for students with additional needs. The SEND Code of Practice 0–25 years has significant impact in terms of this setting. While support systems may already be in place, there may be a need to reassess areas of responsibility. There will certainly be a requirement to adopt new administrative, collaborative and recording mechanisms.
FE college offering mainstream courses – specialist, vocational, academic – and discrete provision for Life Skills/Foundation Tier students and students with learning difficulties and disabilities	While the changes here, as above, are likely to be significant, the expertise and experience of the discrete provision may be an effective source of support. As above, the SEND Code of Practice 0–25 years has significant impact for this setting. Administrative systems will need adoption or amendment but specialist support strategies for vulnerable learners should be available to be shared between the discrete and the mainstream provision.
Special Post-16 institution Independent special college approved under Section 41 of the Children and Families Act 2014	These settings do not require the appointment of a SENCO and systems will already be in place to ensure effective student support. New procedures and administrative systems may, however, need to be adopted in order to fall in line with the ethos of greater collaboration and a multi-agency approach to support. Renewed attention is also required to ensure a student-centred approach.
Vocational learning and training provider in the private or voluntary sector	This setting does not require the appointment of a SENCO and systems should be in place to ensure student support. New procedures and administrative systems may, however, need to be adopted in order to fall in line with the ethos of greater collaboration and a multi-agency approach to support. Renewed attention is also required to ensure a student-centred approach

1 The changing face of special education

In this chapter:

1.1 The purpose of this Handbook

For many years, mainstream schools in England have been required to appoint a Special Educational Needs Co-ordinator (SENCO), although this term was not universally used in schools until the 1980s. The background to the relevant legislation is outlined in sections 1.3 and 1.4.

Although providers of post-16 education are set up in a range of different ways, there has long been an expectation that they will ensure support and guidance for students with learning difficulties and/or disabilities, and this support is scrutinised as part of routine OfSTED inspections. Until 2014, however, the Special Educational Needs and Disability Code of Practice had not extended to young people up to the age of 25. For post-16 provision attached to schools, sixth-form centres for instance, it could be argued that existing practice will have mirrored that of the school itself and, although systems will have been revised to reflect the new Code, this will have taken place from an established starting point.

Colleges and other training providers, on the other hand, embark on this new way of working from any number of different bases. While this could appear daunting, a positive slant can be adopted. The requirements of the Code of Practice set out what providers, and others, must do. It does not, however, describe how it should be done. So, we can be positive about the fact that providers do not have to devise their own obligations because this has been done. It is not the 'what' which needs to be established, it is the 'how': and this book aims to offer practical guidance in order to do this. In this respect, further education (FE) college SENCOs who are new to the role may feel reassured that even those who have been in place for many years are also embarking on new ways of working, adapting to new systems and encountering a range of different outside agencies with whom to collaborate.

This book can be used in a variety of ways. It can be read in order or perused selectively, so as to focus on particular areas of the SENCO role or address particular issues or challenges. At the start of each chapter, an overview of its contents is given to facilitate the speedy location of information and guidance. Chapters contain, where appropriate, Action Points to allow SENCOs to ensure they have not omitted any aspects of their responsibilities. Each chapter ends with a summary of its key points.

Within the chapters, the way in which different styles of provision may adapt and/or introduce systems is set out. In this way, readers may select the part of the guidance that is particularly suited to their setting and their role within it. For instance:

- a sixth-form centre is likely to be designed to incorporate provision for a percentage of learners with disabilities and/or learning difficulties;
- on the other hand, a discrete provision set up solely for the education of these learners should have established specialised systems in terms of staffing levels and expertise and may be able to share these with mainstream colleagues;
- settings which incorporate mainstream vocational and academic courses may lack confidence in the new requirements and need to introduce new ways of working to evidence the support offered to students with additional needs.

It is intended that, when reading in chapter order or by selection of topic, the reader will be able to opt for the section best suited to their needs.

Due to the variety of ways in which education providers and local authorities (LAs) are made up, it has not been possible to provide precise descriptions of how issues should be addressed. Large establishments and LAs may have a dedicated member of staff who undertakes a particular role, while in smaller organisations the role may form only part of one person's responsibilities. Similarly, the manner in which systems are designed and monitored varies between establishments, even within the same LA. For this reason, it is hoped that those with responsibility for the support of young people with learning difficulties/disabilities in post-16 education will identify what needs to be done and use the Action Points in each chapter to assist them in undertaking their role, adapting details and practices as appropriate within the context of their own particular establishment.

1.2 The terminology surrounding special educational needs

A child or young person has special educational needs (SEN) if he/she has a learning difficulty or disability that calls for special educational provision to be made for him/her (Department for Education (DfE), 2014). As the focus of this book is young people aged 16 and over, they will be described as young people and/or students rather than children and/or pupils. This immediately identifies an anomaly with regard to the group of people, including the young person and their family, often referred to as the Team Around the Child because one of the key features of the revised Code of Practice is an emphasis on the person-centred approach to the support of vulnerable young people; this puts the student at the centre of discussions, decision-making and support systems, and requires that the person rather than the team is the key element.

The language used to describe learning difficulties and disabilities, and many other aspects of our culture, has changed and developed over the years and, no doubt will continue to do so. Some terms, previously in common use, appear to us now to be unacceptable and shocking.

Legally, children, here young people, are considered to have special educational needs if they:

> require special educational provision because they have a significantly greater difficulty in learning than the majority of children or of their age or because they suffer from a disability which prevents or hinders them from making use of the educational facilities generally provided for children of their age.
>
> (Department for Educational Science, 1981)

While the term 'special educational needs' is widely used in schools, in FE 'Learning Difficulties and/or Disabilities' is more usually employed to describe the needs of students. A range of such difficulties is described in section 3.3.

As described previously, there is a range of designs for post-16 education and the titles of the professionals working within them are equally diverse.

It is mandatory for mainstream primary and secondary schools to appoint a SENCO and for this staff member to be a qualified teacher. In some schools, this role is combined with that of headteacher, subject or class teacher. However:

> There is no legal duty on colleges to have a SENCO, but colleges should ensure there is a named person in the college with oversight of SEN provision to ensure co-ordination of support
>
> (Department for Education (DfE), 2014)

Table 1.1 Terminology (Pickering, 2005)

Year	**National IQ range**		
	0–25	**26–50**	**51–70**
1913	Idiot	Imbecile	Feeble-minded or high-grade defective
1944	Educationally subnormal (severe)		Educationally subnormal (mild)
1981	Severe learning difficulties		Moderate learning difficulties

… a SENCO by any other name! It is necessary, therefore, for colleges to appoint a staff member to undertake this role. They **may** hold the title of SENCO. Alternatively they may be the Learning Support Co-ordinator, Learning/Student Support Manager, Support Team Leader, Disability Support Co-ordinator, Student Support Co-ordinator or Student Support Manager; the name may differ but the responsibility to ensure co-ordination of support for students with particular needs remains the same. For the purpose of consistency, and brevity, the term used throughout this book is SENCO, with apologies to those who hold other titles.

Terminology in respect of different diagnoses will be discussed in section 3.3

✓ Action

Ensure that, within the organisation, there is clarity regarding overall responsibility for oversight of SEN provision and that management and colleagues are clear about this and about the role they play in the system.

1.3 Background and legislative framework

Historically, it was considered that arrangements for children and young people with learning difficulties and/disabilities should run in tandem with regular schooling so that teaching methods could be appropriately adapted (Burt, 1917). The concept of what is now referred to as 'inclusion' was not on the agenda at that stage. Between 1944 and 1970, however, a series of measures was introduced by successive governments with the aim of raising standards in schools and broadening the equality of opportunity for pupils. It was not until the 1970 Education (Handicapped Pupils) Act that mainstream schools' doors were opened to pupils who may have previously been educated elsewhere.

Probably the most widely known, quoted and discussed document in the field of special education is the Report of the Committee of Enquiry into the Education of Handicapped Children and Young People (Warnock, 1978), more usually referred to as the Warnock Report. The report heralded a turning point in the education of young people and children with learning difficulties and disabilities; they were to be included, if possible, in the mainstream educational provision available to their peers.

The following summary table relates largely to legislation concerning special educational needs in schools. It serves to present a background to the context in which colleges are also situated today.

Table 1.2 Background and legislative framework

1981	Education Act	SEN is given a formal definition Guidelines on assessment procedures Statements of SEN are applied to pupils with significant and/or specific needs
1988	Education Reform Act	Raised expectations of the learning capabilities and potential attainment of young people with SEN Curriculum may be modified or disapplied for pupils with SEN
1993	Education Act	Schools are required to report to parents on systems and provision for SEN Alternative provision for some pupils introduced Appeal procedures put in place
1994	Code of Practice	The Code of Practice introduces a graduated system of categorising the needs of pupils
1995	Disability Discrimination Act (DDA)	DDA requires schools to set out the access arrangements for pupils with disabilities
1996	Education Act	Mainstream schools have a duty to include pupils with learning difficulties/disabilities
2001	Special Educational Needs and Disability Act (SENDA)	Parental rights regarding the choice of placement for their child strengthened Schools required to make reasonable adjustments to accommodate pupils with learning difficulties/ disabilities
2004	The Children Act	Legislative framework for Every Child Matters (ECM), Safeguarding, Common Assessment Framework (CAF)
2005	The Disability Discrimination Act (DDA)	Schools required to prepare and publish a disability equality scheme
2006	Education and Inspections Act	SENCOs in schools required to be qualified teachers
2008	Special Educational Needs (Information) Act	Statistical information regarding pupils with SEN to be published each year

2009	The Education (Special Educational Needs Co-ordinators) (England) (Amendment) Regulations	Schools required to ensure the new SENCO undertakes the nationally approved training to obtain the National Award for Special Educational Needs Co-ordination (NASENCO) within three years of taking up post
2010	Equality Act	Schools to eliminate unlawful discrimination, harassment and victimisation, and advance equality of opportunity Schools to publish information to show compliance, and prepare and publish equality objectives
2013 – 2014	Children and Families Bill The Bill came into force on 1 September 2014 as the Children and Families Act	Extended the SEN system to include those aged 0–25 Those in further education (FE) and training to have the same rights as those in school LAs to publish a local offer of services for SEN LAs and other professionals and partners to work collaboratively to support young people and jointly commission education, health and care services A person-centred approach to be promoted; LAs to consult children and young people with SEN and their parents/carers, if appropriate, in reviewing provision Statements of SEN and Learning Difficulty Assessments to be replaced by Education, Health and Care (EHCPs), focused on outcomes and preparation for adulthood Mediation to be encouraged before going to SEN tribunal Those with an EHCP to be offered a personal budget
2014	Care Act	Collaborative working between agencies Bridges a need for those moving from children's to adult services Features in the Special Educational Needs Code of Practice: 0–25 years

The table above gives an outline of only some of the legislation that relates to the education and support for young people with learning difficulties/disabilities. It is not exhaustive but is intended to give some context and background to the current legislative requirements which affect post-16 education providers.

1.4 The SEND Code of Practice 0–25 years: an overview

While it is interesting and relevant to consider the path of attitudes and legislation set out in sections 1.2 and 1.3 above, it is the most recent developments which directly affect the working of post-16 providers regarding the education of young people with additional needs.

The SEN Regulations 2014 (revised 2015), the SEND Code of Practice 0–25 years, and Part 3 of the Children and Families Act 2014 introduce the greatest reforms to special education for over 30 years (Cheminais, 2015). These reforms are particularly significant for the FE sector as the Code of Practice now extends beyond the age of 16 to embrace young people up to the age of 25.

There are statutory duties placed on post-16 institutions – FE colleges, sixth-form colleges, 16–19 academies and independent specialist colleges – approved under Section 41 of the Children and Families Act 2014. These involve collaboration between education providers, LAs and other professionals, and a greater emphasis on the voice of young people in the decisions taken about their education, health and care. These are set out in detail in **Chapter 2**. Colleges and other providers need to be aware of their statutory duties and SENCOs have the responsibility for translating the requirements into practical systems for implementation. The fact that these duties are based on legislative requirements does, however, raise the profile of the important work to be undertaken in support of vulnerable students.

✓ Action

Become familiar with the legislative requirements that relate to your own setting. In particular Chapter 7 of the revised Code of Practice, which refers to young people in education over the age of 16.

In addition to working with LAs, post-16 education providers are required to adopt new procedures for the monitoring and reviewing of student progress. Statements of Special Educational Needs, which ceased at the age of 16, have been replaced with Educational Health Care Plans (EHCP), which may continue up to the age of 25. Providers are now responsible for reviewing these plans within statutory timescales (**Chapter 7**) and may, in some cases, need to request that a young person has an assessment for an EHCP again, within statutory timescales.

The revised Code of Practice places increased emphasis on the views of the young people themselves and on the outcomes of their education, the aim being to enable them to progress into as productive and independent an adulthood as possible. LAs have, therefore, a duty to ensure that a young person is at the centre of the planning and review procedures. The transfer of Statements to EHCPs is required to be completed by 1 April 2018. Some authorities have transferred all the statements in their jurisdiction at once, others are approaching the transfer in a graduated system and it is useful for the SENCO to become familiar with the progress of the transfers in the relevant authority(s). If the LA has adopted a step-by-step approach, it may be necessary to work with two different systems until the transfers are all completed.

> **✓ Action**
>
> Check the progress of the transfers from Statements of Special Educational Needs to EHCPs in the relevant LA(s).

The points above provide a summary of the focus of the revised Code of Practice and guidance regarding the implementation of these will be given in later chapters.

> A child or young person has SEN[1] if they have a learning difficulty or disability which calls for special educational provision to be made for him/her. Children and young people who have SEN may also have a disability under the Equality Act 2010. Where a child or young person is covered by SEN and disability legislation, reasonable adjustments and access arrangements should be considered as part of SEN planning and review.
>
> (Department for Education (DfE), 2014)

Within the scope of the terms used above, four broad areas of high incidence need are identified:

Table 1.3 Four areas of high-incidence needs

Need	Examples
Cognition and learning	Moderate learning difficulties Severe learning difficulties Profound and/or multiple learning difficulties Specific learning difficulties
Communication and interaction	Speech, language and communication needs Autistic spectrum disorder
Social, emotional and mental health	Withdrawn/isolated/challenging or disruptive behaviours (may reflect underlying mental health difficulties) Attention deficit disorder Attention deficit hyperactivity disorder Attachment disorder
Sensory and/or physical	Hearing impairment (HI) Visual impairment (VI) Multi-sensory impairment (MSI) Physical disability This descriptor should also be considered to include medical conditions such as chronic or even life-limiting illnesses, e.g. cystic fibrosis, asthma, diabetes See also section 2.2

SEN provision is described as additional to and different from that which is provided for the majority of young people. It is underpinned by high-quality teaching but goes beyond differentiated and personalised approaches used for the majority of learners, which is, of course, good practice. Reasonable adjustments (SEND Code of Practice 0–25 years, 3.70) should be made for disabled students to ensure access to the curriculum, extracurricular activities, facilities and information. While accessibility to buildings has been a requirement for some time, the adjustments that in this case could be considered reasonable may take the form, among many others, of additional ramps, hearing loops, rise and fall tables, enlarged resources and so on.

1.5 The role of the SENCO

As described in section 1.2, legislation does not place a duty on colleges to have a SENCO. Colleges and other post-16 providers, should, however, ensure that there is a named person who has oversight of SEN provision to ensure co-ordination of the support given. Here, to remain concise and consistent, this staff member will be called the SENCO.

In some settings, this role may be undertaken by more than one person. It is not unknown for one colleague to oversee the financial and budgetary arrangements for additional provision, while a second colleague is responsible for the practical implications, such as the implementation of support and monitoring of students' progress. This requires, of course, robust collaborative working to ensure that the support offered is well targeted and appropriately resourced.

In schools, the SENCO is required to be a qualified teacher. This requirement does not, however, apply to colleges. It could be argued that an appropriately qualified teacher would be well placed to undertake the responsibilities given in the table below. It could, on the other hand, be proposed that the management of budgets might be more successfully undertaken by a staff member with a background in financial management. Each setting is designed in its own unique way and may choose to allocate responsibility as it sees fit. The important point here is that a robust system must be in place. This must be the overall responsibility of a **named person**, whether or not some aspects are delegated to colleagues with appropriate skills or specialist expertise.

✓ Action

Ensure that there is clarity at all levels regarding who is the staff member with oversight of SEN provision and, where there is delegation, that there are clear lines of communication and responsibilities.

The role of the SENCO can be described as falling into, broadly, three categories:

- assessment and identification
- arrangements for support
- monitoring progress

While these headings may sound simple, each one encompasses a wide range of operational responsibilities.

Table 1.4 The responsibilities of the SENCO

Assessment and identification	Cross-college assessment procedures
	Specific diagnostic assessments
	Consideration of information from schools
	Liaison with specialist assessors, as required
	Consideration of existing Statements/EHCPs
	Applications for assessment for EHCPs
Arrangements for support	Allocation of support staff
	Recruitment of support staff
	Allocation of budgets
	Identification of personal objectives
	Completion of EHCPs
	Communication with colleagues
	Liaison with LA
	Liaison with specialist professionals, e.g. speech therapists
	Training of support staff
	Training of academic colleagues
	Meeting with students
	Liaison with families/care providers
	Feedback to college management
Monitoring progress	Designing/implementing monitoring systems
	Supervising monitoring systems
	Monitoring personalised objectives
	Liaison with support staff
	Liaison with academic staff
	Liaison with specialist professionals
	Meeting with students
	Liaison with families/care providers
	Reviewing EHCPs within statutory timescale
	Feedback to college management

Many of the responsibilities listed in the table above would be considered to be encompassed by existing good practice, for instance liaison with colleagues and monitoring of objectives. Some items have been introduced more recently, however, such as the requirement to review EHCPs against a given, tight, timescale. Guidance on all these topics and suggestions regarding economic yet effective ways of working are given in **Chapter 7**.

Key points from this chapter:

- Use this book in the way most suited to your needs.
- The term SENCO will be used throughout the book.
- Chapter 7 of the revised SEND Code of Practice 0–25 years (2014) focuses on post-16 provision for learners with learning difficulties/disabilities.
- There are three key broad categories to the SENCO's role, each with multiple responsibilities.
- Where delegation takes place, communication and clarity regarding responsibilities are key.

Note

1 The term 'learning difficulties/disabilities' has for some time been used in further education settings, rather than 'SEN'.

2 The Special Educational Needs and Disability (SEND) Code of Practice 0–25 years

In this chapter:

2.1 Outline of the chapter

While legislation has not had a direct impact on the professional practice of those working in further education (FE), they will be aware of the fact that it has, over many years, placed requirements on schools to follow certain procedures. This awareness may result from the experience of friends or family, social awareness and also from working with young people who, while at school, had been diagnosed with an additional need and, perhaps, had a Statement of Special Educational Needs.

Reflection on the path of attitudes and legislation set out in sections 1.2 and 1.3 provides background and context, but mostly it is recent legislative developments which must be considered when working in post-16 education with young people with additional needs.

The SEN Regulations 2014, the SEND Code of Practice 0–25 years and Part 3 of the Children and Families Act 2014 introduce the greatest reforms to special education for over 30 years (Cheminais, 2015). These reforms are particularly significant for the FE sector as the Code of Practice now extends beyond the age of 16 to embrace young people up to the age of 25.

In this chapter, some common descriptors are clarified together with the statutory duties placed on various organisations under the revised Code of Practice.

Local authorities (LAs) are required to publish their **local offer**, a statement of services to be provided. The required content of the local offer is outlined, see sections 2.3 and 2.4 below, so providers may become familiar with sources of information and support regarding their own LA and any others with which they need to liaise and work.

In addition to examining the impact the revised Code of Practice has on SENCOs, it is important to consider what implications it holds for colleagues and for the management of providers. The senior management of any organisation holds ultimate responsibility for its financial stability and for staffing arrangements. Therefore, the SENCO needs to be a key advocate in maintaining the high profile of, and promoting the need to support, the more vulnerable students.

2.2 Definitions and descriptors

As described in section 1.4, if a young person has a learning difficulty or disability that requires for special educational provision to be made for them, they are considered to have SEN. Some of these young people may also, under the Equality Act 2010, have a disability, in which case reasonable adjustments and access arrangements should be considered as part of provision planning and review (Department for Education (DfE), 2014).

Table 1.3 illustrates the four broad categories of the most commonly occurring learning difficulties/disabilities:

- Cognition and learning
- Communication and interaction
- Social, emotional and mental health
- Sensory and/or physical

Within each of these descriptors is, of course, a broad range of ability and disability. It is important to note that, regardless of the severity of the condition, it should not be considered in the same way as a transitory diagnosis, for instance a temporary lack of mobility owing to a fractured limb or routine surgery.

Similarly, as described in section 1.4 there must be clarity regarding the difference between provision which is required to be **additional to/different from** that provided for the majority of a young person's peers and **reasonable adjustments,** including the provision of aids and/or auxiliary services, which may be required to ensure access to buildings and/or the curriculum. The Equality Act 2010 requires that disabled young people are not at a substantial disadvantage compared to their peers and this is reinforced in the Code of Practice 2014 (revised 2015): Introduction xix.

Many young people with learning difficulties/disabilities have more than one diagnosis and it is important to consider each student holistically as an individual rather than assume that a particular condition requires a given support strategy. A student with diabetes, for instance, may also have a moderate learning difficulty (MLD), making the management of the physical condition more problematic. Another student with autism may have a mental health condition that impacts on the strategies chosen to cope with the autistic behaviour and on relationships with others. A learner with a severe learning difficulty (SLD) may also have a sensory impairment which, in turn, necessitates the provision of further strategies and/or resources. SENCOs are offered further information on specific diagnoses in section 3.3.

> **✓ Action**
>
> Ensure that there is clarity regarding the different categories of commonly occurring learning difficulties and disabilities so that this can be disseminated to colleagues within the organisation.

2.3 Statutory duties under the revised SEND Code of Practice 0–25 years

There are statutory duties placed on LAs and on post-16 institutions (FE colleges, sixth-form colleges, 16–19 academies and independent specialist colleges approved under Section 41 of the Children and Families Act 2014) and it is important that there is clarity regarding who is required to do what.

Chapter 1 of the revised Code of Practice describes the principles which should be observed by all professionals who work with young people with learning difficulties/ disabilities. Great emphasis is placed on:

- the views of the young people and their participation in decision-making;
- the collaboration of the partners in education, health and social care in providing support;
- the identification of needs and the provision of high quality support;
- the development of inclusive practices and the preparation for adulthood.

For LAs, the requirements which relate to post-16 provision are that they **must**:

- ensure integration between education and training provision, and social care and health provision to improve the quality of provision for young people with learning difficulties and/or disabilities. These are reciprocal duties and education, health and social care partners must co-operate with LAs on planning, commissioning and reviewing services.
- produce and publish a local offer of services detailing what is available and how to complain if necessary; section 2.4 gives further information about the local offer.
- ensure that there is a graduated assessment process and any decisions regarding education, health or care involve young people and their families throughout.
- after compulsory school age (the end of the academic year in which young people turn 16) the right to make requests and decisions applies to young people directly (Children and Families Act 2014). See sections 8.1 and 8.2.
- transfer Statements of Special Educational Needs and Learning Difficulty Assessments to Education, Health and Care Plans (EHCPs).
- ensure that there is guidance for education and training settings on the support to be provided for young people with learning difficulties and disabilities, in order that their educational goals are achieved and that they make a successful transition into employment and independent living.

Post-16 institutions, as described above, **must**:

- have regard for the Code of Practice;
- co-operate with the LA on arrangements for children and young people with SEN;
- admit a young person if the institution is named in an Educational Health and Care Plan (EHCP); see section 2.4 and also section 7.3 in respect of the right to appeal against decisions made through First-Tier Tribunals, and section 8.1 regarding the voice of the young person;
- use their best endeavours to secure the special educational provision that the young person needs regardless of whether or not the student has an EHCP;
- this duty does not apply to independent specialist colleges or special schools as their purpose is to make provision for young people with SEN;
- under the Equality Act 2010, colleges must not discriminate against, victimise or harass young people with disabilities and must make reasonable adjustments to ensure that they are not placed at a significant disadvantage.

(Further Education: Guide to the 0–25 SEND Code of Practice, 2014, 7.3)

The points above provide a summary of the focus of the revised Code of Practice; guidance regarding the implementation of these will be given in later chapters.

> **✓ Action**
>
> Draw up a clear table of responsibilities, detailing the statutory responsibilities on the part of the LA and those to be undertaken by the education provider.

2.4 Local offer

Every LA is required to prepare and publish a local offer. It must be published on the LA's website but must also be available for those who do not have access to the Internet.

The local offer must include information about:

- the special education, health and social care provision for children and young people with learning difficulties/disabilities;
- details of how young people and parents can request an assessment for an EHCP;
- arrangements for identification and assessment of learning difficulties, including the arrangements for EHCP assessments;
- post-16 education and training provision;
- support for transition;
- support for travel to and from education providers;
- sources of information, advice and guidance in the LA's area;
- young people's rights to appeal against a decision made through the First-Tier Tribunal (SEN and disability);
- the LA's accessibility strategy.

The list above does not include all the requirements of the local offer but identifies those of most relevance to post-16 education providers (Chapter 4 of the Code of Practice contains full details).

In 4.32 of the Code of Practice, LAs, under the heading Education, Health and Care provision, are required to:

- set out a description, covering the authority area, of the special education and training provision it expects to be available in its area, and outside its area, for young people with learning difficulties/disabilities from Early Years to post-16 providers, including funding arrangements and delegated budgets.
- describe the arrangements providers have in place for
  - identification of particular needs;
  - consultation with young people and families;
  - the securing of services;
  - the support available for transition;
  - providing aids and assistive technology;
  - assessing and monitoring progress;
  - securing appropriate expertise among professionals, including professional development.

The local offer must also include directions to information about non-maintained specialist and independent providers who cater for young people with learning difficulties/disabilities, so that students and/or families can, if they wish, take up their statutory right to be named on an EHCP.

The local offer must also include:

- Specialist educational provision, for example learning support services, sensory support services and/or specialist teachers available in the area. Therapies, such as speech and language, and independent travel training specialists should also be listed here.
- Local arrangement for the collaboration between different institutions. This could encompass cluster groups and partnerships as well as arrangements for links between schools and post-16 providers.
- Support systems for young people who have been released from custody, including support relating to education available from Youth Offending Teams.

As before, there are many other areas to be covered in a LA's local offer and here, those of particular relevance to post-16 education providers have been given.

✓ Action

Become familiar with the local offer of the LA (and any others from which students attend) and highlight the areas of particular relevance to their own establishment.

✓ Action

Read Chapter 4 of the Code of Practice and highlight the points which are relevant to post-16 provision and to the SENCO's own organisation in particular.

2.5 Implications for management

The principles underpinning the revised strategy for the support of young people with learning difficulties/disabilities are clear. Education, health and social care providers are to work together collaboratively in a unified system to provide support and care for vulnerable young people. Robust identification strategies and an inclusive approach to the provision of support must be designed to help with the preparation for adulthood. Importantly, the views of the young people themselves are to be given priority in the decision-making process.

None of these admirable principles will, however, be translated into practice without the commitment of the establishments charged with implementing them and this commitment must surely come from the management.

In some cases the SENCO is a member of the management team but in very many others he/she is not. If the SENCO is a member of the management structure, he/she is likely to operate at middle management level; but regardless of whether he/she is in middle management or in another echelon of the organisation, the SENCO must be an informed advocate for the students with learning difficulties/disabilities.

Every department within an establishment has its priorities and wishes these to be placed on the financial and organisational agenda. This can, in turn, lead to conflict as different priorities complete for resources. Senior management, of course, have a responsibility to ensure good outcomes for all students while maintaining a sound financial structure.

The informed SENCO is in a strong position of influence here. While it is hoped that an organisation will not support vulnerable young people merely to remain within the law, an awareness of the legislative requirements regarding these students can be a powerful incentive to ensure their support is appropriate, effective and appropriately resourced.

✓ Action

Ensure that members of the senior management team are familiar with the legislative requirements of the Code of Practice. Particular attention should be paid to admissions, student voice and the ethos that all teaching staff should consider themselves to be teachers of students with learning difficulties/disabilities.

Having provided the management team with the information they need regarding the law, it is important that this remains a priority on the organisation's agenda. In this way, the SENCO can make sure that discussions about staffing levels and expertise, resources and facilities are ongoing. All these areas require financial commitment and this is easier to negotiate if it features as a regular, rather than occasional, item on the agenda.

✓ Action

Request that support for students with learning difficulties/disabilities is a regular agenda item for feedback and discussion at management level.

Management, then, has an important role to play in underpinning the support for young people with additional needs and the SENCO can play a key role in influencing the ethos of their organisation at the highest level. (See also sections 6.1 and 6.2.)

2.6 Implications for SENCOs

As described previously, many post-16 education providers, in advance of the Code of Practice, had well-established systems for supporting students with learning difficulties/ disabilities. Where these is a discrete provision for these learners within largely mainstream provision, SENCOs and staff are well placed in terms of curriculum, staff expertise and resources. The most significant impact for SENCOs in this type of provision relates to administration and procedures.

In mainstream only provision, there is a greater impact. The administration is, of course, to be considered and the requirements regarding assessments, review, collaborative systems and timescales are given in **Chapter** 7. A young person may request that a particular institution be named in their EHCP and the LA must comply with this request unless:

> following consultation with the institution, the local authority determines that it is unsuitable for the young person's age, ability, aptitude or SEN, or that to place the young person there would be incompatible with the efficient use of resources or the efficient education of others.
>
> (SEND Code of Practice 0–25, 7.3)

Young people have the right to appeal against decisions made so it is important that care is taken to ensure that the organisation does not expose itself to the accusation of discrimination against young people with additional needs.

✓ Action

Consider the organisation's admissions policy and consider recommending any alterations required in light of the Code of Practice.

For SENCOs in all post-16 settings, the establishment/maintenance of rigorous assessment and identification of need is fundamental; only when these are in place can support systems be designed and resourced. See also **Chapter 4**: Assessment, Identification and Planning.

✓ Action

Undertake a review of systems for assessment to ensure that they are designed to identify learners' needs.

Review, or introduce, consequential assessments to ascertain specific needs.

Some settings already have a structure which includes a range of support staff (see **Chapter 6**), while for others it is a new requirement and, where this is the case, the support of management, as described in section 2.5, is crucial. It is via the assessment process that the need for a particular type of support is identified; where this is a new feature of the staffing structure, SENCOs should take the opportunity to liaise with other organisations to gather information regarding the management of support systems. This could be via other similar organisations in different areas, local secondary schools or local special schools. The LA should be able to facilitate the making of local contacts. It is often considered to be more positive to present a solution rather than to present a problem. The SENCO may then be able to outline to their management how support staff are organised in settings considered to be successful in this area. This should, in turn, strengthen the presentation of proposed plans for learner support with an enhanced expectation of management support.

✓ Action

Explore, as appropriate, the organisation of support staff systems in other establishments.

One of the greatest impacts of the Code of Practice for SENCOs concerns administration and procedures, and full details of these are given in **Chapter 7**. Statements of Special Educational Needs, now EHCPs, may extend until a young person reaches the age of 25, rather than ending as he/she turned 16. Post-16 providers, therefore, must be aware of the procedures relating to the application for EHCPs, the review requirements and, importantly, the statutory timescales.

The collaborative ethos of the Code requires providers to work in partnership with professionals from a range of disciplines and to place the voice of the student at the core of decisions made about their education. The SENCO, therefore, must adopt and manage review procedures which comply with the requirements and, via liaison with colleagues, ensure that EHCP timescales are met. **Chapter 7** gives full details of the requirements.

✓ Action

Ensure a good understanding of procedures and timescales required by the Code of Practice.

Many students with learning difficulties/disabilities do not have an EHCP. For these learners, appropriate support must also be secured. Depending on the design of the setting, the SENCO must, as described above, ensure that their individual needs are identified and also that appropriate support is made available. This may require the recruitment of support staff, professional development of existing staff, adaptation of resources, acquisition of specialist resources, engagement of external services and, crucially, collaboration with colleagues throughout the organisation (see **Chapter 6**) and management (see section 2.5).

2.7 Implications for colleagues

Where an establishment has a base of expertise in the education and pastoral care of young people with learning difficulties/disabilities, the major implications of the revised Code of Practice relate largely to new administrative procedures, EHCPs replacing Statements of Special Educational Needs, and the requirement for a unified, collaborative approach to working with other professionals. For many, the latter is to be welcomed as a mechanism for eliminating duplication and the potential for information to be misplaced in systems of communication.

For some settings where the majority of provision is academic and/or vocational the implication for the SENCO's colleagues may be more significant. Where learners have specific needs, support may be offered via learning support colleagues tasked with providing assistance on an individual or small group basis, within or outside the teaching sessions. This will require close collaboration between teaching and support staff. Alternatively, learners' needs may be addressed by teaching staff through the use of specialised equipment, greater differentiation in terms of tasks and/or resources and teaching methods.

For colleagues who have had little or no experience of working with young people with learning difficulties/disabilities, there may well be a requirement for professional development, in-house or externally provided. Regardless of the level of previous experience or expertise, communication between support staff, teaching staff and the SENCO must be a key feature of the system as the review of progress towards targets can only be undertaken if it is informed by ongoing feedback from colleagues and from the student him/herself (see **Chapter 6**: Working with Colleagues).

Key points from this chapter:

- There are four broad categories of commonly occurring learning difficulties/disabilities.
- There are statutory duties placed on LAs and also on education providers.
- The SENCO should be familiar with their LA's local offer.
- The SENCO is in a position to keep the support for students with learning difficulties/disabilities as a priority agenda item with management.
- The SENCO's role includes the organisation of support staff, and oversight of feedback and communication systems to inform ongoing review of progress.
- Some colleagues may need support to acquire new skills in the teaching of pupils with learning difficulties/disabilities.

3 Special educational needs in a further education context and the role of the SENCO

In this chapter:

3.1	Outline of the chapter
3.2	What is expected of a further education college/post-16 provider?
3.3	An overview of some learning difficulties/disabilities for which further education colleges may need to design/plan/deliver support
3.4	Colleges that offer mainstream academic and vocational courses
3.5	Colleges that offer mainstream academic and vocational courses, and discrete provision for students with learning difficulties/disabilities
3.6	Sixth-form centres and specialist provision

3.1 Outline of the chapter

Those who work in special education, or who have a child/friend/acquaintance with a special educational need or disability, will be familiar with the role of SENCOs. In primary and secondary schools, this role has been established for many years and people with a particular professional or personal interest have worked alongside SENCOs in a variety of different ways. However, extensive conversations with the wider community and education professionals in the further education (FE) sector reveal that this familiarity is not universal.

Therefore, it is possible, or even probable, that a large proportion of staff in FE settings are unaware of the revised SEND Code of Practice 0–25 years, its implications for them and the fact that the Code now encompasses the education and support for young people up to the age of 25.

It is important at this stage to outline what these implications are for FE colleges and, in particular, the role of the SENCO. The SENCO holds a pivotal position as the professional who sits between the students with particular needs, the college management, outside agencies, families/carers and external professionals. As will be discussed in **Chapter 6** (Working with Colleagues) and **Chapter 8** (Working with Families, Schools and other Professionals), the SENCO must be an informed professional, diplomat and skilled negotiator – taking on the latter role in a range of different contexts!

This chapter, therefore, will offer insight into the expectations of a FE college in light of the new Code of Practice. It is expected that this will, in turn, enable the SENCO to ensure that appropriate support is available for students.

Similarly, an overview of some of the learning difficulties for which a college may need to offer support will strengthen the SENCO's position in conversations with colleagues regarding the nature and structure of support systems required.

In sections 3.4 and 3.5, the opportunities and challenges presented to different styles of college settings are suggested. This will, it is intended, add context but also offer SENCOs the opportunity to develop awareness of college situations other than their own. As a result, SENCOs could cultivate links with others working in equivalent roles within colleges similar to or different from their own. This may be undertaken locally, regionally or on a wider scale in order to share expertise and good practice, for training purposes and for mutual support.

Sixth-form centres and specialist providers will, it can be argued, feel less impact from the new Code of Practice than that experienced by FE colleges. This is due to the fact that the former, if attached to a secondary school, will have existing structures in place which may be continued when pupils transfer at the end of year 11. Admittedly, there are new administrative systems to be adopted as a result of the transfer of Statements of Special Educational Needs to Education, Health and Care Plans (EHCP), but the basic arrangements and systems for the co-ordination of support are already in place.

Similarly, specialist providers already have expertise and experience in the organisation and delivery of support to students with a range of diverse needs and, like sixth-form centres, they need to make adjustments to some administrative practices.

Sixth-form centres and specialist providers may, therefore, experience less impact from the new Code of Practice than that felt by FE colleges. The value of shared expertise and experience must not be undervalued, however, and SENCOs in colleges should find it useful and profitable to develop contacts with specialist centres and providers in their area, as well as with organisations in the voluntary sector that specialise in various learning difficulties and/or disabilities.

3.2 What is expected of a further education college/post-16 provider?

There was an existing requirement that students in FE should receive appropriate support for any learning difficulties/disabilities and this has, for many years, been monitored via the inspection system. However, the Children and Families Act, 2014 and the revised Code of Practice have important implications for post-16 settings in respect of students with such difficulties. The Code places emphasis on the preparation for adulthood which should underpin the learning of young people with learning difficulties/disabilities. Some students transferring to post-16 placements will have had Statements of Special Educational Needs that were intended to secure appropriate additional support for their learning in school, but these Statements will have ceased as they left school at the end of Year 11. However, the Act and the Code bring together the pre- and post-16 systems for young people with learning difficulties/disabilities into one system and new duties are placed on FE providers. See section 2.3, on statutory duties.

With the increased emphasis on the involvement of young people in the decisions made about their education, health and care, they are now in a position to name a particular institution in the EHCP. (Code of Practice, 9:78) The local authority (LA) is obliged to name the institution in the EHCP plan unless, according to the Code of Practice (7.79):

- it would be unsuitable for the age, ability, aptitude or SEN of the child or young person, or
- the attendance of the child or young person there would be incompatible with the efficient education of others, or the efficient use of resources.

While section 2.3 outlines the statutory duties imposed on education providers, section 7.3 summarises the situation regarding appeals against decisions taken as the revised Code places greater emphasis on the voice of the young person (see also section 8.1).

Colleges are expected to be ambitious for young people with learning difficulties/ disabilities and should provide support at all levels to promote good outcomes for them. The young people should have access to a wide range of study programmes, including short programmes. This applies to students from Entry Level upwards but not to students on Higher Education level courses.

It is important to remember that requirements and expectations apply to learners with learning difficulties/disabilities whether or not they have a Statement of Special Educational Needs or an EHCP.

Colleges and training providers should ensure that students are on an appropriate course and use their best endeavours to ensure that the necessary provision is made for any student who has a learning difficulty/disability. Information from the students' previous education providers may be very useful to colleges when assessing the type and level of support they require.

Colleges will, of course, need to undertake their own assessments with students but these may be informed by previous records or reports. Information received will not, however, be of a uniformly high standard or may not be forthcoming at all. The college, via the SENCO, will need therefore to ensure that timely identification of needs is made in order to facilitate access to the curriculum. See **Chapter 4** (Assessment, identification and planning and **Chapter 9** (Planning for transition).

At this stage there may be a requirement for the new setting to manage the expectations of both learners and their families/carers; while educators, students and their families/ carers will aspire to the highest attainment, unrealistic expectations will lead to failure to achieve, loss of self-esteem and, in fact, narrow the options for further progress. The conversations surrounding the management of expectations will require considerable interpersonal skills, tact and diplomacy on the part of the SENCO, particularly if there is a mismatch between the findings of the setting's assessment strategies and the aspirations of the learner and/or their family/carers. See also **Chapter 8** (Working with families, schools and other professionals).

After initial assessment and the identification of need have taken place, the SENCO needs to plan the support required by individual learners. In order to draw up a meaningful Individual Learning Plan (ILP)/Individual Education Plan (IEP)/Personal Learning Plan (PLP) the SENCO may need to 'translate' the outcomes set out in the EHCP. It is equally important, of course, that relevant and meaningful plans are also put in place for learners without an EHCP but who are found to have additional needs. Colleges may receive EHCPs from a number of different LAs. What should be in EHCP plans is set out in the Code of Practice but they will vary in design, quality and clarity depending on the originating LA. The SENCO needs to ensure that they are purposeful, measurable and accessible to the colleagues who will be working with the learners. See **Chapter 4** (Assessment, Identification and Planning) and **Chapter** 7 (Administration and procedures).

3.3 An overview of some learning difficulties/disabilities for which further education colleges may need to design/plan/deliver support

If appropriate and effective provision is to be planned and delivered, it is important that there is an understanding regarding the type of difficulty experienced by young people with learning difficulties/disabilities. In order to ensure that teaching and support colleagues are appropriately informed and skilled, the SENCO must develop as broad an awareness as possible of potential challenges presented to, and by, students with different difficulties.

As described in section 2.2, the areas of particular need which may be identified before embarking on post-16 provision, via assessments at the new setting or during the progress of the new course/training, fall into four broad categories:

Cognition and learning

- Many students with **moderate learning difficulties** are accommodated in mainstream provision with appropriate support while others flourish in a setting (discrete or stand-alone) designed specifically for their development.
  - These learners are unable to access learning at the same pace and to the same level as their typically developing peers.
  - They will require a range of different types of specialised support to enable them to acquire skills, dependent on the nature and level of their difficulty.
- Specialist provision is, for the most part, more suitable for students with **severe learning difficulties** and learners with **profound and/or multiple learning difficulties**. Highly specialised teaching and facilities should be available in these settings to support the complex needs of the learners.
- **Specific learning difficulties** refers to learners who have, as the term suggests, difficulties in a specific area. This is not to say, however, that they may not co-exist – for example, dyslexia and dyspraxia – and more complex support packages may be required for young people who experience difficulties in more than one area.
- High incidence **specific learning difficulties** are:
  - **dyslexia**, which is primarily concerned with a difficulty in acquiring literacy skills;
  - **dyscalculia**, which involves a difficulty in acquiring numeracy skills;
  - **dyspraxia**, which is associated with co-ordination, affecting fine and/or gross motor skills.

Communication and interaction

High-incidence examples of communication and interaction difficulties include:

- **Speech, language and communication needs**; included here are learners who:
  - experience difficulties in **producing** fluent speech;
  - have difficulties in **processing** the spoken expressions of others.
- **Autistic spectrum disorder (ASD)** (includes Asperger syndrome)
  - Autism is often described as a 'spectrum disorder' as the condition affects people in a variety of different ways and to varying degrees.
  - People with ASD can be described as having a condition that affects social interaction, communication, interests and behaviour.
  - People with ASD have difficulty in understanding other people's feelings or emotions.
  - People with ASD find it hard to initiate conversations and/or to take part in them.
- People with **Asperger syndrome (AS)**
  - Asperger syndrome is a form of autism and people with AS have difficulty in expressing themselves socially and emotionally.
  - People with AS find it difficult to read the body language and/or the facial expressions of others and to recognise the personal space of others.
  - People with AS may be very literal in their understanding and may be unable to understand metaphor, jokes etc.
  - Change of routine or order may be distressing and challenging for people with AS.

Social, emotional and mental health

Difficulties in this area manifest themselves in many ways including:

- being withdrawn or isolated;
- displaying disruptive and disturbing behaviour;
- hyperactivity and lack of concentration;
- immaturity in relation to social skills;
- challenging behaviour.

The list above is not exhaustive but offers some common characteristics of learners with social, emotional and mental health disorders. The behaviours above may be attributed to:

- attention deficit disorder (ADD);
- attention deficit hyperactivity disorder (ADHD).

Some behaviours may also reflect an underlying

- mental health disorder including depression, obsessive–compulsive disorder, self-harm, bipolar disorders, eating disorders;
- attachment disorder.

Sensory and/or physical

Learners may have, or develop,[1] conditions that include:

- hearing impairment, ranging from slight impairment to profound deafness;
- visual impairment, ranging from partial impairment of sight to total blindness;
- multi-sensory impairment – impairment or limitation of more than one of the senses;
- physical disability, which encompasses a range of difficulties including:
  - mobility
  - impairment of gross motor skills
  - chronic and or life-limiting medical conditions such as:
    - epilepsy
    - diabetes
    - asthma
    - cerebral palsy
    - multiple sclerosis
    - muscular dystrophy
    - motor neurone disease
    - chronic fatigue syndrome
    - cancer

Again, the examples above do not provide an exhaustive list, but serve as a reminder of some of the most high-incidence difficulties/disabilities with which a young person may present. If a young person with any of these challenges is to receive appropriate and effective support, colleagues need to be aware of and equipped to address the needs of the student in question.

✓ Action

Develop an overview of the most commonly occurring learning difficulties/ disabilities and what is required to offer support.

The levels of staff experience and knowledge of different needs will, of course, vary and, in order to plan robust support for students, it is important to establish what these are. This will, in turn inform the planning of professional development and the deployment of support staff.

✓ Action

Undertake an audit of teaching and support staff to establish levels of awareness, skills and experience of working with young people with a variety of different challenges.

3.4 Colleges that offer mainstream academic and vocational courses

It is in this provision that, perhaps, the greatest change has taken place in relation to the accommodation of students with learning difficulties and/or disabilities. Of course, in the climate of inclusion colleges have been expected, where possible, to include and support learners with additional needs. However, before the introduction of the revised Code of Practice, a Statement of Special Educational Needs ceased to apply when a pupil left school at the age of 16. The revised Code of Practice imposes the continuation of the statutory support while the young person continues in education up to the age of 25. The Statement of Special Educational Needs has been replaced by the EHCP which seeks to draw together all the support agencies involved with the young person.

The SENCO in this setting has the responsibility of ensuring that students with particular needs receive the appropriate level and type of support. This is not a new requirement but should be found in existing good practice. The most significant changes are to be found in the administration of and accountability for this support. EHCPs, detailing the preferred educational establishment, needs and challenges, and outcomes and goals for individual learners must be reviewed to statutory timescales. Close liaison with the LA and other professionals involved with the learners is of paramount importance in this process to ensure a joined-up approach to the support of the young people. The students themselves now have a louder voice in relation to their education and care and the voice of their families/carers takes a lower priority; this may require considerable diplomacy on the part of the SENCO should there be a disparity between the views of the student and their family/carers (see sections 8.1 and 8.2).

✓ Action

Establish and develop a strong, collaborative working relationship with the relevant colleague(s) in the LA.

The role of the SENCO, then, is multifaceted. They must be the strategic leader of the systems in place to support students with particular needs, representing them at senior management level. They must be an adviser, supporting colleagues who are embracing new approaches in their teaching, as well as providing/facilitating and advising on continuing professional development (CPD) where appropriate. They must be an agent of collaboration between previous education/care providers, the LAs (often, several different LAs) and the college. They must be an advocate, representing the young people with learning difficulties/disabilities both within their setting and beyond. Lastly, they may need to be the bridge between student and family/carers where aspirations differ or expectations require management.

3.5 Colleges that offer mainstream academic and vocational courses, and discrete provision for students with learning difficulties/disabilities

All of the points above (section 3.4) apply in colleges that offer mainstream academic and vocational courses, and discrete provision for students with learning difficulties/disabilities. There are, however, additional nuances to be considered in a setting which offers these two different levels of provision.

The discrete provision for learners with particular needs provides an in-house source of expertise that may be shared with mainstream colleagues. While the students receiving the discrete provision are likely to have greater needs than those on mainstream courses, the staff who work with them are an invaluable resource in terms of specialist knowledge and expertise. The SENCO can negotiate the dissemination of this knowledge and expertise in a number of ways: one-to-one training for mainstream staff working with a student who has a particular need, departmental training for colleagues who feel ill-equipped to support the needs of some learners and cross-college training (INSET/college development days) where the profile of learner support and strategies for implementation can be shared.

Assuming that the SENCO and the manager of the discrete provision are not the same person, they need to work in close collaboration. This will facilitate the sharing of knowledge and expertise, as well as the smooth running of administrative procedures. Additionally, cross-departmental links will be fostered, with both staff and students being able to experience the work of and life in other areas of learning.

✓ Action

Set up an ongoing, non-competitive pattern of liaison with the manager of the discrete provision with the intention of developing skills amongst mainstream staff via in-house training and development (formal and informal).

3.6 Sixth-form centres and specialist provision

Many sixth-form centres are attached to secondary schools. For this reason, they find themselves in a continuum of provision which extends from the school into the sixth form. Secondary schools, while having the need to adapt procedures to accommodate the requirements of the revised Code of Practice, have systems and strategies in place which place them in a strong position to meet the new statutory requirements. Certainly, new administrative systems and deadlines need to be accommodated but the basic structure of support should be in place. Similarly, the expertise of staff is available and should be readily accessible across age groups in order to secure professional development for colleagues working with students with learning difficulties/disabilities. The Year 7–11 SENCO may be the same person as the post-16 SENCO, in which case, systems can be streamlined. If this is not the case, the post-16 SENCO can fruitfully develop and maintain a mutually informative relationship with the Year 7–11 SENCO in order to benefit from the expertise of colleagues, opportunities for professional development and streamlining of systems.

✓ Action

Establish robust transition strategies for pupils transferring from Year 11 to post-16 departments/centres. This should include links between settings in terms of information, staff and learners.

Settings which offer bespoke education for learners with a range of, or specific, difficulties will have specialist staff, teaching and support in place in order to enable their learners to access the curriculum, develop social and life skills, and plan for adult life. In these settings, there will already be an ethos of 'every teacher is a teacher of special educational needs'. It is the new administrative procedures and timescales that are more likely to be noticed here. The member(s) of staff charged with the maintenance of systems should, by working closely with LAs, be able to adopt the new structures and, as required over time, amend and develop them.

Key points from this chapter:

- It is expected that post-16 education provision for learners with learning difficulties/disabilities will maintain high expectations and provide appropriate support to promote good outcomes for them.
- Within four main categories of need, there is a very wide range of challenges for which learners need support in varying degrees. SENCOs should have a broad knowledge of these in order to plan appropriately to meet students' needs.
- SENCOs should liaise with colleagues within their organisation, including managers of discrete provision, to facilitate the development of appropriate skills and ensure smooth transition.
- SENCOs should undertake an audit of existing knowledge, skill and experience in different areas of difficulty in order to plan professional development to support learners' needs.

Note

1 It is important to remember that while a learner may arrive in their new educational setting with a pre-existing diagnosis, it is possible that, in some cases, a difficulty has not previously been identified. It is also possible for a condition to develop during the student's time in the setting. This may be as a result of a trauma, accident, illness or deterioration/increase in symptoms. Some conditions are life-limiting and in all cases the necessary close liaison with health care professionals – and, where appropriate, a young person's family/carers – will require sensitivity. SENCOs must make certain that any changes in a student's health or treatment are communicated to all appropriate colleagues to ensure informed consistency.

4 Assessment, identification and planning

In this chapter:

4.1 Outline of the chapter

4.2 Information received from schools

4.3 Assessment at post-16

4.4 Identification of additional needs – areas of need
(i) Students with an EHCP
(ii) Needs identified via assessment

4.5 'Labels'

4.6 The rights of the young people

4.7 The graduated approach – planning and implementation of support

4.8 Working in partnership

4.1 Outline of the chapter

In this chapter a crucial element of post-16 education will be considered. Appropriate support can never be identified and provided unless the needs of each individual learner are assessed. Only then can plans to overcome challenges be put in place alongside strategies to enable the students to access learning and move forward.

Robust assessment methods will be discussed and also the need for ongoing vigilance and analysis of need. Information from schools and local authorities (LAs) may provide some insight into a particular learner's strengths and areas for development. However, it is important to remember that some difficulties may not have been previously identified and that others may develop as a result of illness, trauma, accident, social circumstances and numerous other causes.

4.2 Information received from schools

It might be expected that the most reliable source of recent information regarding the ability and needs of a students would be provided by the secondary school last attended. In an ideal world this would certainly be the case; sadly, this is not universally the reality.

Many schools are able to furnish informative accounts of a learner's history, including their strengths, their challenges, the type of support that has proved successful in the past, and details of their social and family circumstances. Others provide little or no background.

Some would argue that the information received from schools is invaluable as a basis for planning support in the new setting. Others believe that a new setting should provide a new start with any 'history' being left in the past.

It is sensible and practical to adopt both sides of this argument! Phrases such as 'can display a bad attitude and is reluctant to work collaboratively with his peers' and 'fails to appreciate the importance of time management' can indicate something – but what?

In the first case, one or more staff members have found it challenging when requiring the student to work with others

- Was this all staff?
- Was it in some or all lessons?
- Did this relate to certain peers?
- Were any strategies implemented to overcome this?

The second student was, it would appear, a poor timekeeper.

- For every lesson?
- At the start of the day? Is this related to home circumstances or travel arrangements?
- After breaks? Is this a peer-related issue?
- Does this relate to particular lessons, situations?
- Is the student able to tell the time accurately?

Given the questions arising from the information provided by school, it is important for the new setting, while taking account of this information, to engage in a thorough and robust series of assessments of its own. In this way, some background history may shed light on the results of assessments, while deeper analysis may highlight areas where strategies to enable the student to overcome some challenges are required.

If a student has an Education, Health and Care Plan (EHCP), it will contain information about the assessed needs of the learner and goals towards which he/she is working (see also section 7.2). At the post-16 stage, these plans may have been compiled from a number of different LAs, depending on where the young person was previously educated. This may present the new setting with some challenges; the statutory content of the EHCP must be covered but the design and clarity of the Plans will vary. The Plans must be reviewed to a statutory timescale (section 7.5) and staff will need to receive guidance from the SENCO regarding the nature of the support required by individual students. For this reason, it may be necessary for the SENCO to 'translate' elements of the EHCP to create purposeful, meaningful, appropriate and measurable targets with which the students and staff members can work (**Chapter 5** and section 7.4).

4.3 Assessment at post-16

Question: What is the best method of assessment when a student starts their education in a post-16 setting? **Answer**: How long is a piece of string?

It could be argued that one of the main reasons for initial assessments is to meet the requirement that students are enrolled on the appropriate course. No professional educator would want a learner to embark on a pathway on which they had no chance of success. So the object of the exercise is to make sure that the course is appropriate for the learner and, importantly, any support they may need to succeed on that course is identified so that plans may be put in place to facilitate this.

There are numerous assessment strategies that can be employed by colleges and training providers, most of which have strengths and shortcomings. Online, computer-based assessments are accessible and, as the marking is undertaken by the computer, popular with many staff. The drawback of these, however, is the potential for 'happy clicking', where a student loses interest, guesses or is distracted, thus giving a potentially misleading result. This sort of assessment also places students who have problems with gross and/or fine motor skills at disadvantage.

Many colleges and providers combine the computer-based assessments mentioned above with free-writing and paper-based literacy, numeracy and/or vocational exercises to provide a fuller picture of the learners' strengths and the areas in which they are likely to struggle.

The move from secondary school to college, apprenticeship or another training provision is, for any young person, a big step; moving from the status of schoolgirl/boy to that of student and the challenges that this brings should not be underestimated. The transition from the security of the familiar environment (even if this was not one in which the learner felt comfortable and secure) to a larger, unfamiliar setting is a major stepping stone. It is crucial that staff in the new setting take the time to get to know their new intake, via formal assessments, but it is just as important that they do so through opportunities to observe and discuss their initial progress.

Colleges and training providers will have established, over time, an assessment policy which is utilised with new learners to establish literacy, numeracy, social and other skills. It may be necessary for the SENCO to introduce further assessment methods in order to identify specific needs.

✓ Action

Review the establishment's assessment policy and assessment strategies. If necessary, develop or acquire additional assessment tools that are accessible to learners with particular challenges.

It is crucial that assessment is not a one-off, start-of-course procedure. It is entirely possible for needs to have been overlooked or misinterpreted previously. It is also possible for challenges to develop over time. So, for instance, while a new learner may have undiagnosed dyslexia, another may suffer a deterioration in sight or hearing during their course. Equally, illness or trauma may introduce a new difficulty not previously experienced. It is important that colleagues, therefore, are vigilant for the causes of poor achievement and/or changes in behaviour or physical difficulties.

✓ Action

Undertake an audit among colleagues to assess awareness of indicators of physical and learning difficulties.

✓ Action

Provide training for all staff on the identification of physical and learning difficulties as part of establishment-wide development, e.g. development days, INSET.

4.4 Identification of additional needs – areas of need

It has been established, then, that there is no single 'magic wand' which will identify the needs of individual students as they embark on their new educational pathway. Information that may come from schools and formal assessments that are made, as well as more informal observational strategies, will all serve to build a picture of the needs of any given learner.

It is perhaps appropriate to mention at this point that in many cases information received beforehand or emerging as a result of assessment may require 'reasonable adjustments' to be made. Organisations must, legally, have policies to ensure that access to buildings and facilities is available. Other adjustments may involve rise-and-fall tables for wheelchair users, the provision of hearing loop systems, facilities to enlarge resources and so on.

4.4(i) Students with an EHCP

On arrival, some students will be in possession of an EHCP, which should detail their individual needs, challenges and goals.

Colleges and other providers are likely to admit students from a number of different LAs and it would be fair to say that the style and quality of EHCPs may vary. This presents a challenge for the admitting college, and in particular the SENCO. The goals in the EHCP may be meaningful and clear and thus transferable to the student's ILP/IEP. It is possible, however, that the outcomes in the Plan will be less well defined and will need 'translation' in order that the student and all the staff working with them can relate to meaningful, realistic and achievable goals. This presents an additional challenge for the SENCO but is highly instrumental in ensuring that both the student and the staff with whom they work are clear about overall aims and the steps required to achieve them. The requirements and timescales in respect of EHCPs will be outlined in **Chapter** 7.

4.4(ii) Needs identified via assessment

It is not uncommon that, during the initial assessment process, the need for support is identified and that this needs further scrutiny. Staff may become aware of a learner's difficulty in literacy and/or numeracy and this may be the trigger to enlist the expertise of colleagues.

For many conditions it is necessary for a specifically qualified professional to undertake the assessment. Many school pupils with specific difficulties will have had the involvement of, for instance, an educational psychologist (EP) to inform their diagnosis. If dyslexia is suspected, a colleague qualified via the British Dyslexia Association (BDA) must be the professional involved in assessment. Larger establishments may have a staff member who holds the BDA qualification, but where this is not the case liaison with other local organisations may facilitate access to a suitably qualified professional. Of course, in the latter situation the services of an external practitioner to undertake an assessment will involve a financial implication. The benefits of sharing expertise within localities and specialisms cannot be overstated and the development of local, regional and national networks has proven to be rewarding and mutually beneficial.

✓ Action

Establish whether or not there are organisational colleagues with the necessary qualifications to undertake specific assessments. If appropriate, liaise with other local providers to share expertise.

As described in section 4.3 above, it is important that assessment is not considered to be a one-off task to be undertaken at the start of a student's post-16 educational experience. It should involve ongoing vigilance so that difficulties may be identified at any stage.

Whether needs are identified before, at the start of or during a learner's post-16 education, SENCOs need to arrange appropriate support for individual students. This may be through existing knowledge and experience, professional development for staff or, in some cases, the recruitment of appropriately trained staff.

In some instances, a college or another post-16 provider will decide that a young person should be assessed for an EHCP and has the right to request such an assessment. This should be with the knowledge and agreement of the young person where possible; the SEND Code of Practice 0–25 years (2014) places the young person at the centre of discussions and decisions regarding his/her needs. This is particularly significant at the post-16 stage of education and students may decide, at this point, that they do not wish their parents/carers to be involved.

It could be argued that, if a need exists, an EHCP should have been requested and put in place at an earlier stage. However, the need may be identified at the post-16 stage if, for instance, the high level of support provided by the learner's school setting is not available in the college or the other provider's existing provision. Alternatively, a request may be made due to the development of a physical or learning difficulty which was not previously identified. As described earlier, accident or illness may also lead to the need to request an assessment for support which was not required earlier.

4.5 'Labels'

It is important to bear in mind that a student who fell behind at school or who is identified in the new setting as struggling to achieve does not necessarily have a learning difficulty/

disability. They may have one but this should not be assumed. There are numerous causes for underachievement including social circumstances, health issues, anxiety about family members, frequent change of schools and prolonged absence. It is necessary to consider all the possibilities, including a learning difficulty/disability, when assessing and planning support. Should it be identified that there are other reasons for the learner failing to make the progress expected, they will still require support, short or long term, and colleagues and other professionals may need to be involved. In some cases, a 'fresh start' approach can herald greater achievement than had previously been the case and the information from schools, mentioned in section 4.2 above, can offer a historical view of a learner who may, in fact, thrive in a new setting.

✓ Action

Ensure that pastoral systems are robust in order that all potential causes for underachievement may be considered.

There are differences of opinion relating to the positive and/or negative effects of assigning a 'label' to the needs of a young person. It is argued that singling a learner out and attaching a descriptor to them is not inclusive, may be isolating and can stigmatise the student. Others prefer to attach an 'explanation' for particular challenges. Dyslexia or attention deficit hyperactivity disorder (ADHD) may be preferred to 'poor reader' or 'badly behaved'. Although the discussion around labels cannot be fully explored here, it is important to bear in mind that, in many cases, the identification of a difficulty can be used to attract additional resources, financial and practical, and lead to greater awareness of the nature of the support likely to be useful to the young person.

Where the diagnosis of a chronic medical condition has been made, the 'label' can be considered as a vital indicator of the type of support and intervention required. This is also a guide to the range of other professionals involved with the learner. Under the umbrella of the EHCP, professionals from a number of disciplines should be able to work collaboratively to support the well-being and progress of the young person.

4.6 The rights of the young people

The revised Code of Practice (2015) places greater emphasis on the rights of young people and their families/carers. After compulsory school age, the right to make requests and decisions under the Children and Families Act 2014 applies directly to the young people, rather than to their parents/carers. It is to be hoped, and experience indicates, that in the majority of cases, families will continue to offer support with the making of decisions or, in fact, act on behalf of the young people – but this can only apply if the young people are happy for this to take place.

Young people can, then, request a place at the establishment of their choice; where there is an EHCP in place, the LA must name the establishment on the Plan and require that appropriate 'reasonable adjustments' are made. One of the expectations of a further education (FE) or training provider is that they ensure their students are enrolled on a suitable course at an appropriate level and that they use their best endeavours to make certain that learners are offered the right type and level of support to progress. Where there is a mismatch of aspirations versus realistic outcomes, considerable diplomacy is required on the part of the SENCO, who may need to have sensitive conversations in order to manage the expectations of the young people and/or their families/carers.

Colleges and other post-16 providers will have existing policies about the involvement of families/carers and this would normally include their level of involvement should there be concern about the progress and/or behaviour of the learners. 'The fact that the Children and Families Act 2014 gives rights directly to young people ... does not necessitate a change to a college's safeguarding or welfare policy' (Department for Education (DfE), 2014).

A young person is also among those who may request an assessment for an EHCP and may request the provider's support in going about this. As previously mentioned the post-16 setting can request an assessment and, ideally, the young person and the provider would work together to take this request forward. See section 7.3.

4.7 The graduated approach – planning and implementation of support

Many will be familiar with the cycle: **assess, plan, do, review**. The cyclical approach is widely adopted and recognised as good practice in the creation and implementation of policies across a wide range of professional situations.

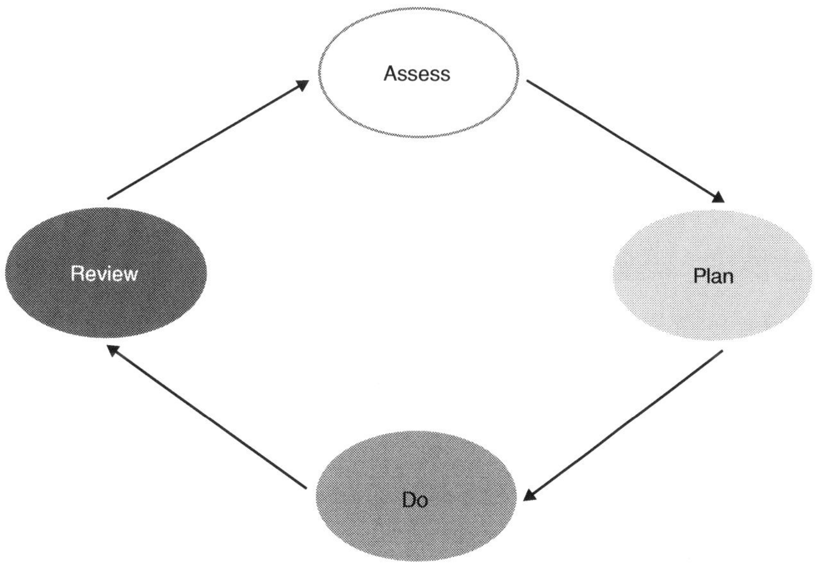

Figure 4.1 Assess, plan, do, review

> ✓ **Action**
>
> Audit systems of cyclical review across the organisation.

When planning support for learners, the SENCO needs to work in partnership with the students' subject tutor/personal tutor. The subject tutor remains responsible for working with the learner on a regular basis. Where interventions involve one-to-one or group teaching away from the subject tutor, they should still retain responsibility for the student. The SENCO should support the subject tutor/personal tutor in identifying the learners' individual strengths and challenges, and advise on the implementation of support.

✓ Action

Publish guidelines for new and existing tutors to establish their responsibility for supporting learners with additional needs.

High-quality, differentiated teaching should be the first step in supporting learners who may have a learning difficulty/disability. Where students continue to make poor progress despite high-quality teaching, the subject tutor should work with the SENCO in order to assess whether the young person has a significant difficulty. Tutors may need targeted continuing professional development (CPD) to ensure that they have an understanding of strategies for supporting vulnerable young people.

✓ Action

Survey levels of tutor confidence in the support of learners with learning difficulties/ disabilities.

For higher levels of need, colleges and other providers should have arrangements in place that allow them to access more specialised assessments, if necessary from external agencies and professionals.

An effective graduated approach could be said to comprise several key elements:

- leadership that promotes an ethos of high expectations and an inclusive climate;
- an ethos wherein all tutors contribute to the approach;
- a consistent cross-setting approach;
- a person-centred approach where the students' views are considered;
- a SENCO who is prepared and equipped to support colleagues;
- continuing professional development (CPD) designed to improve every tutor's ability to adapt teaching to respond to the needs of all students.

4.8 Working in partnership

Whether assessment is undertaken entirely within the setting or external expertise is required, the SENCO needs to work in close partnership within and outside the setting. The LA is required to publish its local offer, giving details of what every young person with learning difficulties/disabilities can expect from their education. The local offer must be published on the LA's website and arrangements must be made to enable people without Internet facilities to access the information.

EHCPs must be regularly reviewed (See section 7.5). This may involve working with a range of different professionals from LAs, health services, education and social care. Strategies should be in place to enable liaison to take place effectively and technology can be a useful tool to ensure this.

✓ Action

Identify key personnel in the LA and other sectors with whom to liaise to support learners with learning difficulties/disabilities.

SENCOs need to work in partnership with their colleagues (section 4.7, above) to draw up and monitor effective support strategies for students with learning difficulties/disabilities. Colleagues with little or no experience of working with young people with additional needs will need considerable support and CPD in order to develop a greater knowledge and a wider skill set (see **Chapter 6**).

The most important partners in the arrangements for young people with particular needs must be the learners themselves. As we have seen, at the age of 16, students have the right to make requests and decisions about their circumstances and, while the family/carers may be involved if the young person agrees, this is not always likely to be the case. The involvement of families/carers and the rights of the young person to decide on their level of involvement are examined in section 8.2.

Key points from this chapter:

- Information from previous education providers can be useful but may vary in quality/quantity.
- Formal assessment tools each have advantages and disadvantages.
- A combination of different assessment methods can be useful.
- For specific learning difficulties, a suitably qualified assessor is required.
- Assessment is not a one-off procedure to be undertaken at the start of a course. Staff should be vigilant for previously unidentified difficulties and/or those which develop over time.
- The SENCO should be aware of the expertise, experience and confidence among teaching staff in relation to learners with learning difficulties/disabilities and their support.
- The SENCO should ensure that appropriate training for colleagues is integral to the organisation's staff development agenda.

5 Identifying and managing support needs

In this chapter:

5.1 Roles and responsibilities

As discussed in the previous chapter, subject tutors/personal tutors and SENCOs have a key role to play in the support of students with additional needs. They are not, however, the only adults who work with young people in a post-16 setting. Many colleges and other provisions employ additional support staff and it would, perhaps, be useful here to establish some clarity regarding different roles and their descriptors.

Different establishments use different titles for support staff and understanding of these titles varies. Here, for clarity, the terms Teaching Assistants (TAs), Learning Support Workers (LSWs) and Personal Care Assistants (PCAs) will be used although other nomenclature may be used for similar roles in different settings.

Teaching Assistants are often allocated to a particular group of students. They work closely with the Personal Tutor and Subject Tutors to offer support as directed by the tutor in class. They may be asked to work with individual learners or with small groups as required. They are often employed in areas of a setting with larger numbers of students requiring additional support and discrete provision: for instance, for learners with learning difficulties/disabilities. Due to the fact that TAs spend so much time with the same group of young people, they are an invaluable source of information for colleagues. For this reason, they can also provide feedback for reviews and reports. However, it is important to remember that they are employed to assist, not deliver, the teaching and that different colleagues may choose to deploy them in different ways in class depending on the subject or environment. TAs are normally part of the provision's staff compliment and are funded from the setting's budget for students with particular needs.

Learning Support Worker is the term more often used for a staff member who is assigned to support the needs of specific individual students rather than a whole group. This may be to assist with a physical disability, a more profound learning difficulty or a specific learning difficulty (SpLD). One student is likely to work with several different LSWs during the course of a week. For some support needs it is very important that the LSW is appropriately qualified. Learners who need assistance with transferring from a wheelchair, for instance, should receive this from a staff member trained to do so and some LSWs may be trained to also offer personal care. The funding for LSWs varies according to the setting. In some cases a pool of core staff make up a bank of LSWs to be allocated to students as appropriate. Other specifically qualified LSWs may be recruited to meet the needs of individuals. The support may be provided via an Education, Health and Care Plan (EHCP) where a one-to-one relationship has been identified as necessary. In some cases this support may be funded from a **personal budget** (SEND Code of Practice 0–25 years, 3.38).

Personal Care Assistants, like LSWs, work with individual students to deliver assistance in relation to personal care. This may be funded from a personal budget and should be identified on an EHCP. Both LSWs and PCAs are in a position to offer feedback on areas of progress for the learners with whom they work, again offering an invaluable source of information.

Specialists from within and outside the setting may also work with the young people. In-house dyslexia specialists, for instance, are a great asset in the support of students with dyslexia and also in recommending support strategies to colleagues. Speech therapists, independent travel advisers, diabetes nurses and physiotherapists are further examples of specialists who may work with young people with learning difficulties/disabilities to enhance their ability to move forward.

5.2 Different support for different needs

After the initial assessment period and consideration of all the information provided about and by the young person, the appropriate type and level of support must be identified. Each learner's needs must be individually considered in order to provide the most appropriate strategies. The type and level of support will be affected by the nature of the setting in which the student is placed. For example, in a mainstream setting, one-to-one assistance may be required, while this may not be the case in a special, discrete setting where the staff to student ratio is weighted and groups are smaller. In all settings it is paramount that careful consideration of the type and extent of individual support must be made, with a focus on the interests of the young person and their thoughts and feelings on this.

✓ Action

In advance of the start of the academic year (during recruitment for new students) undertake an audit of the support needs of all students with learning difficulties/disabilities.

✓ Action

Compare the needs of the students with the skills and experience of existing support staff, including specialisms, to inform any staff recruitment issues.

In a **mainstream setting** the SENCO will consider:

Table 5.1(i) Support staff in mainstream settings

Q Does the learner have a difficulty which requires one-to-one support in all lessons?	Does this support require a particular specialism, e.g. signing?
Q Does the learner have a difficulty which requires support in some lessons?	Does this support require a particular specialism, e.g. dyslexia?
Q Could support be offered to a number of students in the same session by one member of staff?	Does this staff member need particular expertise, e.g. behaviour?
Q Will the support be delivered most effectively within the session or by working individually or in small groups outside the session?	
Q Does the learner have an EHCP? **YES**	• What does the student think would be supportive and helpful? • How does the student feel about their need for support and how it should be delivered? • What strategies have been successful in the past? • Is sufficient funding available? • Does the student have a personal budget to support these strategies? • Are there appropriately trained/experienced staff to meet these needs? • Is an external specialist – e,g. a speech therapist, diabetes nurse or physiotherapist – required to offer regular therapeutic support? How will this impact on the timetable of the learner? • Is there a need to recruit staff with a specialism, e.g. signing?

Table 5.1(i) Continued

Q Does the learner have an EHCP? **NO**	• Do we have information from school to inform support plans? • How does the student feel about the support they need? • Will the learner need one-to-one support in all sessions? • Will the learner need one-to-one support in some sessions? • Would the learner benefit from a TA being present in all sessions? • Would the learner benefit from a TA being present in some sessions? • Is there a need to recruit staff with a specialism, e.g. signing? • Can support for the learner be provided within existing budgets? • Is there a need to request an assessment for an EHCP? • If yes, see section 7.3

In a setting with a **discrete provision** the SENCO will need to consider:

Table 5.1(ii) Support staff in discrete provision

Q Does the learner have a difficulty which requires one-to-one support in all lessons?	Does this support require a particular specialism, e.g. signing?
Q Does the learner have a difficulty which requires support in some lessons?	Does this support require a particular specialism, e.g. dyslexia, autism awareness?
Q Could support be offered to a number of students in the same session by one member of staff?	Does this staff member need particular expertise, e.g. behaviour, communication and interaction difficulties, cognition and learning difficulties?
Q Will the support be delivered most effectively within the session, or by working individually or in small groups outside the session?	

Table 5.1(ii) Continued

Q Does the learner have an EHCP? **YES**	• What does the student think would be supportive and helpful? • How does the student feel about their need for support and how it should be delivered? • What strategies have been successful in the past? • Is sufficient funding available? • Does the student have a personal budget to support these strategies? • Do we have appropriately trained/experienced staff to meet these needs? • Is an external specialist – e.g. a speech therapist, diabetes nurse, physiotherapist – required to offer regular therapeutic support? • How will this impact on the timetable of the learner? • Is there a need to recruit staff with a specialism?
Q Does the learner have an EHCP? **NO**	• Is there information from school to inform support plans? • How does the student feel about the support they need? • Will the learner need one-to-one support in all sessions? • Will the learner need one-to-one support in some sessions? • Would the learner benefit from a TA being present in all sessions? • Would the learner benefit from a TA being present in some sessions? • Can support to the learner be provided within existing budgets? • Is there a need to request an assessment for an EHCP/personal budget? • If yes, see section 7.3

5.3 Staff specialism, recruitment and deployment in different styles of provision

As a result of the assessments, resulting questions (above) and discussions, plans must be made to ensure that the appropriate arrangements are made for support. It is probable that, in mainstream provision, subject/vocational tutors and personal tutors will need support, training and CPD to help them to provide the appropriate and individual access to learning required by some of their learners – a factor which is further discussed in **Chapter 6**. This is no reflection on the professionalism of the colleagues involved but rather an acknowledgement that, for many, their path into the world of further education (FE) may not have equipped them to address such a diverse range of learners.

In discrete provision it is more likely that teaching colleagues have experience and expertise in a broad variety of additional needs, although further training and development can also be beneficial here. In both mainstream and discrete provision, support strategies and staff will need to address the areas of high-incidence need identified in the Code of Practice 2015 (6.26–6.35) and described in sections 2.3 and 3.3 of this book.

In the stage of learner recruitment and induction where provision of support is planned, however, it should be the SENCO's prime concern to ensure that, where staff additional to the teaching complement are considered necessary, these staff are in place, appropriately skilled and fully informed about the students they are tasked to support.

Larger post-16 education providers with an existing support-staff establishment are in the fortunate position of having a pool of staff to draw upon and deploy as required. The challenge for the SENCO is to make sure that there is a match between supply and demand. As explored in section 5.1, there are numerous ways in which support staff are arranged, equipped, trained and experienced. The role of the SENCO is to make sure that these invaluable resources in terms of staff are deployed to maximum benefit.

With reference to Tables 5.1(i) and 5.1(ii), the SENCO is required to be a strategic co-ordinator in order to make sure that the support needed by each individual learner is matched by the resources available. The ways in which this can be put into practice are many:

Teaching Assistants allocated to particular groups/sessions

This may be on a whole-week basis or a session basis, e.g. for practical/written/off-site sessions.

Learning Support Workers allocated to individual students

This may be on a whole-week basis or a session basis, e.g. for mobility/behavioural support in given situations such as off-site sessions, written work, or for learners with sensory limitations.

Personal Care Assistants allocated to individual students

This is likely to be for assistance with transfer, mobility, motor skills and toilet arrangements.

External specialists to work with individual students

To assist with, for example, speech therapy, independent travel, assistive technology ... The SENCO, in this case, must ensure that arrangements are made for the learner and the specialist to be available to one another with minimum disruption to the student's timetable for learning. Students with medical conditions such as cystic fibrosis, asthma or diabetes may also receive support from appropriate specialists or may require regular medical appointments. Again, the SENCO must ensure access to this support in and/or outside college time while endeavouring to ensure minimum disruption to the learner's timetable.

Some settings may not be in a position to deploy existing support staff to assist students who have been identified as requiring additional help. This introduces the necessity for recruitment or additional staff CPD. SENCOs in establishments with an existing support-staff base may also find themselves in the position of needing to recruit additional staff or offer professional development to staff to meet new or specialised needs.

The decision to recruit or offer CPD will, it must be acknowledged, be partly dependent on budgetary constraints. For this reason, it is imperative that the SENCO keeps the issue of support for learners with learning difficulties/disabilities as a high-profile agenda item with the management of the establishment in order to secure sufficient resources.

If a decision to recruit additional staff with the required specialism is made, this may be on a limited contract to meet the need of the student and accommodate the time he/she will spend in the setting. For instance, if a student with a hearing impairment is on a two-year course, the staff member recruited to provide signing assistance is likely to be employed on a short-term contract.

Table 5.2 Considerations for recruitment of support staff

TA required to support a group/session	From existing staff complement? • Yes – deploy, making arrangement with departmental staff/ timetables • No – Recruit, on short-term contract – Within constraints of budget – Training to be given as necessary
LSW needed to support individual student(s) in some or all sessions	From existing staff complement? • Yes – deploy, in collaboration with departmental staff • No – recruit on short-term contract – Within constraints of budget – Via EHCP – Via use of personal budget
PCA required to support personal care of student	• It is likely that this care arrangement is already in existence and funded from a learner's personal budget or under an EHCP – Discussion with departmental colleagues is required in order to facilitate the smooth operation of support/additional arrangements

The required content of an EHCP is detailed in section 7.2 and all staff who work with a student with such a Plan should be aware of its content and stated outcomes. It has already been mentioned that it may be necessary for the SENCO and other colleagues to 'translate' the outcomes set out in an EHCP into manageable and relevant targets for weekly/monthly/termly feedback. All students, with or without an EHCP, should have their own agreed plan of outcomes. Each setting will have its own format of ILP, IEP or similar document. It is important that each member of staff working with a student is familiar with the content and objectives of this in order to ensure a consistent approach to a mutually understood outcome.

✓ Action

Having audited learner need and compared this with support staff available, recruit any additional staff, with appropriate specialisms if required.

✓ Action

In advance of the student starting a course, liaise with relevant external specialists to ensure that systems are in place for the learner to access the support needed, with reference to his/her timetable.

5.4 Budgeting for the support of students

All school and academy sixth forms, sixth form colleges, FE colleges and 18–19 academies are provided with resources to support students with additional needs, including young people with SEN and disabilities (Code of Practice, 7.28).

The establishments mentioned above receive, based on a national funding formula, an allocation of funds to deliver their core provision. Additional funding is allocated to support students with additional needs but this is not ring-fenced and is included in the main allocation. Colleges are expected to provide high-quality support for students with additional needs using all the resources available. The ethos of the establishment will, therefore, be of the upmost importance in the budget planning process and this will determine the organisation's approach to the use of resources in respect of the support of young people with learning difficulties/disabilities. The governors and senior management of the organisation should establish and publish their approach to the support of these learners in the context of their total available resources. This will enable them to issue their offer of what students and their families/carers can expect regarding provision of support for learners with additional needs (see sections 6.1 and 6.2). Personal budgets may be available to learners with Education, Health Care Plans (Code of Practice, 3.38). However, feedback from local authorities (LAs) and SENCOs indicates that the take-up of these has been very limited.

When more expensive support is required, colleges are not expected to provide this from their allocation (Code of Practice, 7.32). There is a nationally prescribed threshold (per student, per year) up to which they are expected to provide support. Where the cost of the special provision exceeds this threshold, LAs should provide the 'top-up' funding. This will normally be the LA in which the young person lives. As SENCOs in post-16 education settings are likely to work with young people from more than one LA, this will involve liaison and collaboration with colleagues from outside the immediate geographical locality, each with their own differing systems. Working with management will be discussed in section 6.2 and procedures and administration in **Chapter** 7. However, here, the importance of the management's commitment to the support of young people with additional needs and the need to foster collaborative relationships with key personnel in LAs cannot be overstated. The SENCO has a pivotal role to play in both these relationships, not just as the expert/authority on statutory requirements, but as a strategic advocate and champion, and a skilful negotiator.

Key points from this chapter:

- There are a number of differing styles of support staff deployment that can be made available to learners.
- It is important that the needs of individual students are identified in a timely fashion so that appropriate support can be arranged.
- The levels of expertise and specialist knowledge in teaching and support staff should be audited so that the deployment of support can be managed effectively.
- It may be necessary to recruit additional support staff to meet learners' needs; this may be on a short-term contract.
- Close liaison with external specialists, such as medical professionals, is required.
- SENCOs should work closely with the management to ensure additional needs and their funding remains a priority

6 Working with colleagues

In this chapter:

6.1 Context

One of the certainties relating to the role of the SENCO is the requirement to be a pivotal player when working with colleagues within and outside the organisation at all levels of responsibility. As described previously, the government is a key influence on the requirements and expectations of a setting. However, the management (sections 2.5 and 5.4) is a key influence on the priority and importance given to these and on the ethos of an establishment regarding attitudes to the support for students with learning difficulties/disabilities.

In addition to being the advocate for these students at management level, the SENCO must also work to ensure that, at teaching and additional support level, appropriate measures are taken to ensure that the learners receive the resources they need and that appropriate strategies are employed to facilitate their progress. Liaison with teaching staff will involve a number of different elements, depending on their training, experience, approach and outlook. Colleagues employed specifically to support students with additional needs may themselves need training and development in order to learn new skills or develop awareness of particular needs, strategies or conditions.

Communication within and outside the organisation is crucial and, in order to ensure that information is shared in a format which is accessible to all relevant parties, a one-page

Profile is a useful method through which to share information. This can be developed with the learner, whose voice is an important aspect of the ethos surrounding the support for young people with additional needs. A Profile may give information about the likes and dislikes of the student and their long- and short-term aspirations. Their strengths and challenges should be detailed, together with the support they have received in the past and their feelings about this. This simple document, when shared with colleagues, teaching and non-teaching, will be highly instrumental in planning future support and in sharing information. If regularly reviewed, it will also provide a useful tool for successful onward transition and preparation for adulthood.

The SENCO will inevitably need to work with colleagues from different local authorities (LAs), the local LA and with specialist professionals engaged to offer assistance to learners with specific needs. LAs are organised in a range of different ways and outside agencies also have particular systems in place. A challenge for SENCOs is to become familiar with the various ways that the agencies with which they must work communicate and the key personnel with whom they need to engage.

6.2 Working with management

It has been established that the governing body (GB) and senior management team (SMT) of an educational setting are crucial in the approach taken to meeting the needs of learners with learning difficulties/disabilities. 'The principal or a senior leader should establish a clear picture of the resources available to the college and consider their strategic approach to meeting SEN in the context of the total resources available' (Department for Education (DfE), 2014). It is evident, then, that decisions regarding resources will be taken at the highest level of management.

Governing bodies in schools, colleges and other post-16 education providers represent the local community and offer a wide range of knowledge and experience. Some members will have a background in or experience of working within an educational setting. All members will have experienced education, locally or elsewhere, and will have valuable contributions to bring to the overall management of the setting.

Governing bodies and SMTs must be aware of their strategic responsibilities via the SEND Code of Practice 0–25 years, but there is a difference between an ethos born from a statutory requirement and one which reflects a genuine desire to support the most vulnerable young people according to their needs. Some members of the governing body and the SMT may have knowledge regarding what is involved in providing the wide range of support required to enable these vulnerable learners to access learning, but this will not universally be the case.

This is where the SENCO needs to be an advocate, a facilitator and a negotiator. The needs of the learners and the practical strategies involved in their support must be represented. The implications in terms of resources, staffing and training must be outlined. Importantly, the determination to further the development of vulnerable young people, and the allocation of resources to support this, should not be understated. The SENCO may instigate discussions which raise ideas that challenge traditional arrangements. For instance, would some learners with learning difficulties/disabilities flourish within a different time structure such as shorter weeks and shorter holidays? Is a five-day week, with a long break in the summer, in the best interests of some learners? If timetables were implemented in a different way, what would be the implications for staff and resources?

It can be an advantage if the SENCO is part of the management team. As a team member, they will have access to those colleagues who hold responsibility for resourcing, prioritising and planning. If the SENCO is not part of the management structure, strategies must be devised to ensure that not only is management aware of its statutory obligations but also that the issues relating to young people with learning difficulties/disabilities are kept on the agenda and treated as priorities.

✓ Action

Deliver training to the senior management team and governing body on their statutory obligations and also on the implications for practice and resources.

This will not only raise awareness but also keep the issue of support for learners with learning difficulties/disabilities as a priority agenda item.

✓ Action

Encourage members of the governing body and senior management team to attend whole-establishment development sessions (development days/programmes, INSET) on topics relating to the support of learners with learning difficulties/disabilities.

6.3 Teaching staff – qualifications; all teachers are teachers of SEN; training implications

In schools, as stipulated by the Code of Practice (2014), the SENCO must be a qualified teacher. It is also now mandatory that the school SENCO should undertake the National Award for Special Educational Needs Co-ordination (NASENCO) within three years of taking up their post; this is a master's level (Level 7) award. In the further education (FE) setting there are no such requirements, either for the SENCO to be a qualified teacher or for the NASENCO qualification. It is possible, therefore, that those who hold responsibility in areas concerning the support of students with learning difficulties/ disabilities may have no background in teaching and/or no qualification relating to teaching or special educational needs. This may affect the SENCO's credibility when working with qualified teaching staff, advising them on procedures and requiring them to accommodate new ways of working.

✓ Action

Consider undertaking the NASENCO award qualification, especially if no other relevant qualification is held (see also section 6.5).

Teaching staff in post-16 educational settings bring with them a wide variety of backgrounds, experience and qualifications. Some colleagues may have qualifications and/or experience relating to school teaching e.g. a first degree plus Postgraduate Certificate in Education (PGCE). In vocational areas, it is more likely that a staff member will be an experienced practitioner in their subject with a wealth of skills to pass on to their students. These will relate to a vast range of different topics or subjects, each with its own specialist learning outcomes and some, but not all, colleagues will have undertaken a PGCE or Certificate in Education (Cert Ed) in order to develop the skills required to pass on their expertise to their learners. Some establishments make it a requirement that teaching staff undertake these qualifications as a condition of their employment. Other qualifications include assessors' awards, which equip staff to measure the skills and knowledge of learners while following a vocational or practical course of study.

Unless the colleagues in question have a PGCE (Primary or Secondary) qualification, it is likely that any teaching qualification held will have been studied on a part-time basis. This includes Qualified Teacher Learning and Skills (QTLS) status which is acquired via the provision of evidence of teaching work undertaken on an ongoing basis. In each case colleagues should have benefited from advice and guidance from course tutors and mentors but, necessarily, the time available for focus on specialised aspects will have been restricted; discussion with current and past students of these qualifications reveals that study relating to learning difficulties/disabilities will, as a result, have been limited or not included at all.

The Code of Practice is committed to the approach that all teachers are teachers of SEN. For this reason, it is expected that subject tutors will be encouraged to perceive themselves in this way. This is where there can be a considerable task for SENCOs to undertake. There may be no lack of willingness on the part of subject/vocational tutors to offer support to students with learning difficulties/disabilities, but there may be a lack of knowledge and experience and, therefore, confidence on their part to do so. In some cases, there may also be a reluctance to engage in new strategies and methods in order to accommodate the needs of some learners.

So, the SENCO may, then, be faced with a scenario where teaching colleagues are willing, but ill-equipped to support young people with learning difficulties/disabilities and there may be others who feel that responsibility for this area should, in fact, be left to the SENCO and support staff to manage. The attitude of the latter group of colleagues can be changed by skilful negotiation, especially if the management of the setting is supportive of this approach. Colleagues need to be given confidence in their role and in the tools with which to carry it out. In both the scenarios mentioned here, there is a clear need for professional development and training and the SENCO can be highly effective in identifying the knowledge and experience their colleagues require and facilitating the delivery of this.

Training and development may be delivered in a number of different ways. Establishments commonly hold training days, when single or multiple topics are made accessible to all staff. If there is a setting-wide need, this is a good opportunity to ensure that all staff receive the training: autism awareness, for example. If this can be delivered by existing staff members, the SENCO or colleagues from a discrete specialist area, this is also a cost-effective system of development.

There may be occasions when particular tutors, because of their student cohort, would benefit from specialist training and development not available in the setting. Courses, attendee and online, on a variety of topics are available in most areas and nationally, and links to further information regarding this are given at the end of the book. If individual staff members are given the opportunity to attend or take part in training, there is a chance for setting-wide benefits to take place via colleague dissemination of skills and knowledge acquired.

What, then, are some of the approaches that teaching staff need to employ when working with learners with learning difficulties?

Table 6.1 Approaches to teaching learners with learning difficulties/disabilities

Cognition and learning		
	Students with moderate learning difficulties may be unable to access the curriculum at the same pace as their peers	High-quality differentiated teaching and resources are essential to accommodating a variety of ability levels Additional staff may feature in this support
Specific Learning Difficulties (SpLD)		
Examples of SLD are		
Dyslexia	Difficulty in acquiring literacy skills	Dyslexia can only be diagnosed by a qualified assessor. Specialist support may be required to assist learners with SpLD.
Dyspraxia	Difficulty with co-ordination, affecting fine and/or gross motor skills	Appropriately skilled support staff may be able to assist with some aspects of these difficulties
Dyscalculia	Difficulty in acquiring numeracy skills	
Communication and interaction		
Speech, language and communication difficulties	Difficulty producing fluent speech Processing the spoken language of others	Specialist speech therapy may be required. Staff should liaise with specialist staff to develop the skills to offer consistent support
Autistic spectrum disorder (ASD), including Asperger syndrome (AS)	Autism is often described as a 'spectrum disorder' as it affects people in a variety of ways and to varying degrees	Care must be taken to become familiar with the exact nature of the difficulties experienced by individual learners

Table 6.1 Continued

	Learners with ASD and AS have difficulty understanding other people's feelings or emotions. They often find it hard to initiate conversations and/or to take part in them	Ensure that the nature of this aspect is known to colleagues, and peers, in order to avoid the assumption of rudeness
	Learners find it difficult to read the body language and facial expressions of others	Ensure that verbal communication is clear and unambiguous as this may be the only aspect of conversation processed by the learner
	Learners may find it difficult to recognise the personal space of others	Repeatedly remind learner of the need to respect the personal space of others. Ensure that colleagues and peers have an understanding of this aspect of the learner's difficulties to avoid potential confrontation
	Many people with ASD are very literal in their understanding and are unable to understand metaphor, sarcasm, jokes etc.	Make sure that verbal and written communication is clear, literal and without scope for any potential misunderstanding or offence
	Change of routine or order may be distressing and challenging for people with ASD	Prepare learner for any changes to routine, e.g. trip, change of room, change of staff. This should be done clearly and, if possible, well in advance of the change
Social, emotional and mental health		
Attention deficit disorder (ADD)	Learners find it difficult to maintain concentration and/or focus	Break instructions, tasks and activities into small steps, requiring that the learner need only focus for a short time before moving onto the next step
		Vary tasks frequently
		Be prepared to repeat instructions regularly throughout a task to assist the learner in remaining on task
		Use a variety of prompts to support focus on the task in hand, e.g. verbal, written, pictorial etc.

Table 6.1 Continued

Attention deficit hyperactivity disorder (ADHD)	In addition to the difficulties experienced by those with ADD, learners with ADHD display overactive and impulsive behaviour with little or no regard for consequences	The strategies suggested for young people with ADD should also be employed for those with ADHD Ongoing reminders about behaviour should be given in a sensitive and supportive manner Some learners benefit from a sanction and reward strategy to assist them to develop the skills to manage their difficulties; where this is employed, care should be taken to ensure that colleagues are consistent and that peers are aware of and understand the reasons for the strategy Some learners find the need to 'take five' when they become stressed about a particular task. Staff can develop a system whereby a potential episode is spotted and thus avoided. Learners themselves can also be encouraged to recognise when tension is building and a mutually agreed signal can be exchanged. Care must be taken that, where the 'take five' strategy is used, this system is not abused by a learner who uses it to remove him/herself from a session at will. Appropriately skilled support staff can be instrumental in supporting learners with ADHD, to keep them on task, monitor stress/behaviour levels and accompany them, if appropriate, while they leave the session to regain control of their behaviour.

Table 6.1 Continued

Mental health and attachment disorders	These may manifest themselves in many ways including withdrawn or isolating behaviour, disruptive or disturbing behaviour, immaturity in social skills and challenging behaviour	Where a mental health or attachment disorder is suspected, discussion should take place with an appropriately qualified professional colleague. This expertise may exist within the organisation or it may be necessary to involve the services of external professionals When working with a student with mental health disorders, it is vital that staff are aware of the learner's challenges and the triggers that might exacerbate these
Sensory and/or physical difficulties		
With sensory and/or physical difficulties, the range, as described in section 3.3 is extensive in terms of challenges and levels of severity. As a result the knowledge and skills required to support these are wide-ranging. Each learner must be considered individually and their needs assessed. In this way the SENCO will be able to ensure that colleagues are appropriately skilled and confident to support the learner. If this is not the case, appropriate training to meet specific needs can be arranged.		

The approaches suggested in the table above are, of course, not comprehensive and each learner and staff member must be considered individually. The table does, however, outline a few of the skills and strategies that staff can consider when working with individual students with particular difficulties and some sections also suggest training implications. As will be seen in section 6.5, there are numerous ways in which training may be delivered and skills acquired.

✓ Action

Undertake an analysis of staff training needs. This should be done regularly to include new staff and reflect the current cohort of learners.

✓ Action

Develop a programme of training for teaching staff on their role in relation to the support of learners with learning difficulties/disabilities.

This should include generic training to be delivered across the setting, bespoke sessions as required, and information about external and online courses.

✓ **Action**

Provide or arrange one-to-one training for individual colleagues on aspects of support in which they feel that they are lacking knowledge, experience and confidence.

6.4 Support staff – qualifications, expertise and specialism

It has already been established (see section 5.1) that colleagues from inside and outside the setting may be known under a range of different titles and may be involved with a number of different support responsibilities.

External colleagues such as speech therapists, diabetes nurses, educational psychologists are qualified specialists in their fields, and their training and development is not the responsibility of the educational setting.

However, with regard to support colleagues within the establishment, the SENCO must be aware of the needs of the learners, the skills needed by those supporting them and, in turn, any training and development required to ensure that the needs of the learners are met.

6.4(i) Teaching Assistants

Where Teaching Assistants (TAs) are allocated to groups of pupils, they should be operating under the direction of the class/subject/group tutor. In FE, this means working with a number of different tutors teaching a particular group. It is important that time is available for direction and feedback before and after sessions, as the progress of the learners must be monitored closely. In this area, the SENCO has a responsibility to ensure that systems are in place for this to happen and that they are operating effectively. As discussed in section 6.3 above, the SENCO may need to call on leadership and diplomatic skills here, depending on the attitude and experience of teaching colleagues, and the skills and expertise of support staff.

In 2009, the findings of the Deployment and Impact of Support Staff Project (Blatchford, et al.), commonly referred to as the DISS Report, were published. Although the Project focused, over five years, on support staff in schools there are strong parallels in relation to post-16 education. The key messages from the Report relate to the deployment of support staff and the clarity of roles. The impact on learning is central and the SENCO has a key responsibility here to ensure that this clarity is in place and that deployment supports the learning of the students.

The SENCO will need to evaluate the effectiveness of TAs to ensure that OfSTED's criteria for effective deployment of TAs are met. While the descriptors below refer to schools, they may be a useful framework for post-16 SENCOs when considering the evaluation of the support for learners with learning difficulties/disabilities.

As Cheminais (2015) outlines, OfSTED will award a grade of:

- **Outstanding (1)** if they consider that TAs make a significant contribution by supporting learning and well-being, and providing a wide range of learning support opportunities. Importantly they will comment on the extent to which TAs are well directed to support learning.
- **Good (2)** if they consider that the TAs relate well to the learners they support and have high expectations of them. They will also make a judgement as to effective deployment of TAs.
- **Requires improvement (3)** if they consider that there is inadequate use made of TAs and that learning is not supported due to lack of understanding and low expectations.
- **Inadequate (4)** if they consider that poor management has caused ineffective use of TAs and/or that they contribute little to learning and well-being due to lack of understanding, knowledge and skills.

✓ Action

Ensure that all teaching staff, and TAs, are aware of the descriptors above, encouraging them to seek advice, support or training if necessary.

While the criteria above refer to TAs, they could also be used/adapted for the evaluation of other support workers, e.g. Learning Support Workers (LSWs).

In 2003, a qualification for TAs to become Higher Level Teaching Assistants (HLTAs) was introduced. This is a Level 4 qualification and is offered by many universities, colleges and other training providers. TAs are able to evidence and develop their skills, expertise and experience and to receive an award for this. Many establishments are keen to support TAs though this process. It cannot be overstated, however, that TAs may find it difficult to embark on the HLTA journey without the support, financial and practical, of their organisation. Here, the SENCO can be instrumental, if necessary, in supporting their TA colleagues and negotiating, at management level, their development opportunities. Once again, the ethos of the establishment and the attitude to the support of students with learning difficulties/disabilities is key in these discussions. The SENCO is in a prime position to ensure that the high-quality support of vulnerable learners is considered a high priority, if this is not already the case.

6.4(ii) Learning Support Workers

If the setting is fortunate enough to have a bank of support workers – referred to here as LSWs – the SENCO should be in a position to allocate individual staff members to meet specific student needs.

The ways in which LSWs are required to support young people with learning difficulties/disabilities are numerous (see also **Chapter 5**). Note taking, dyslexia support, behaviour support, signing, mobility and personal care are a few of the areas in which learners need assistance. There may be occasions, both in larger and smaller establishments, when skills/expertise of existing staff do not match the specific needs of learners. Training may resolve this mismatch, but if the specialist training is too long for a staff member to undertake in order to meet the requirements of an incoming learner, there may be the need to recruit colleagues with existing specialist qualifications, for example signing.

The SENCO is in a position, via the application process, to alert the organisation to the upcoming students' needs and should be highly involved, as the staff member with overall responsibility for support, in the recruitment process. The full-/part-time nature of the specialist's employment and its contractual length will depend on the needs of the learners

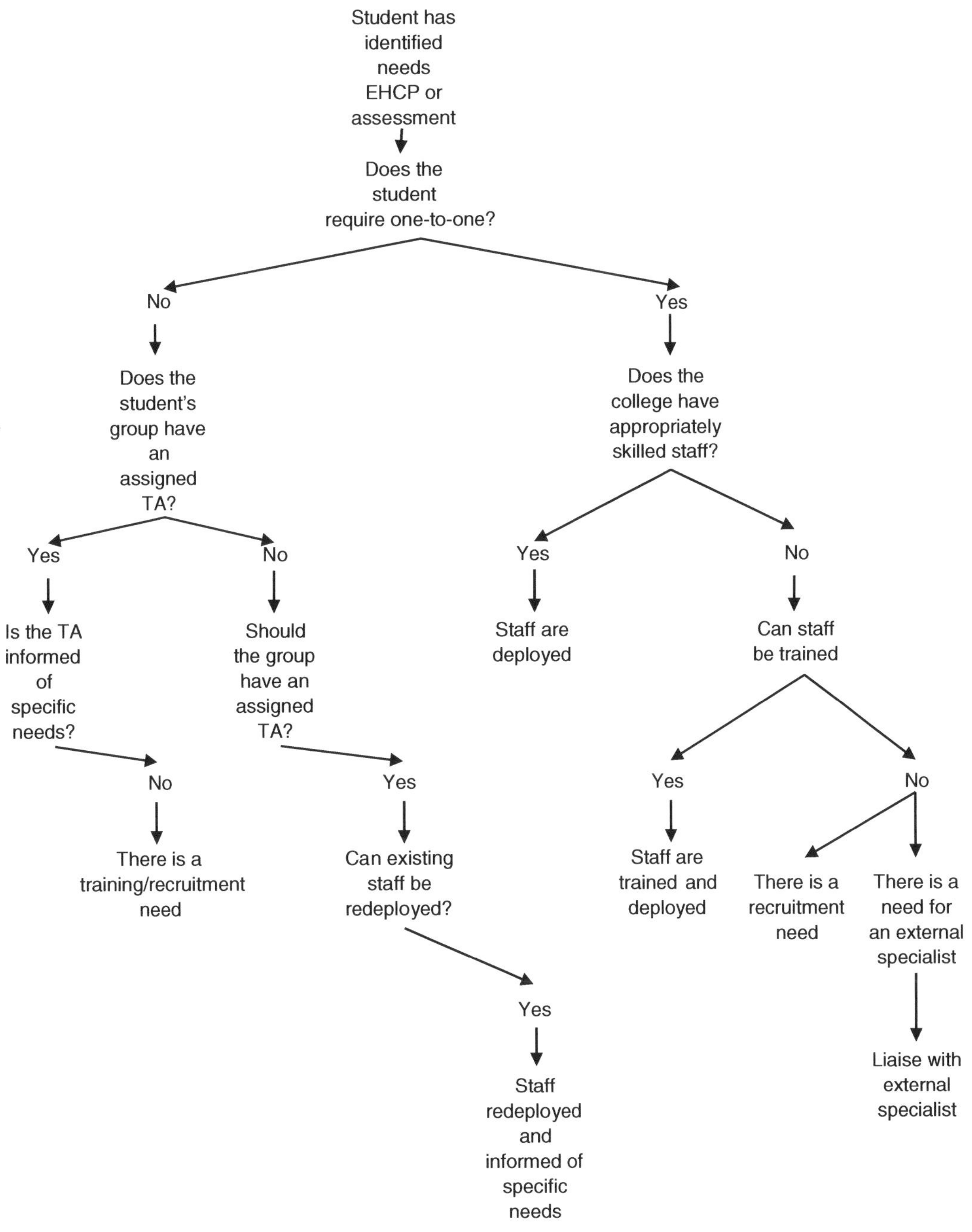

Figure 6.1 Learning support flowchart

and of the establishment; furthermore, specialists may have other skills which affect the nature and length of their contract.

When it comes to the support available from external professionals it is difficult to offer specific guidance as LAs and local arrangements are organised in different ways and SENCOs will find themselves operating in different situations. However, the key colleague in the external field is the LA officer who has responsibility for young people with learning difficulties/disabilities in the local area. In some LAs, this will be a colleague dedicated to post-16 students, in others they may be involved with learners from pre-school through to post-16 education. Forging strong links with the LA makes for the smooth progress of many aspects of the SENCO role (see **Chapter 7**) and will also facilitate contact and relationships with external agencies, such as mental health services, speech therapy specialists, psychologists, independent travel advisers and health professionals.

A key point to bear in mind when deciding on the deployment of TAs and LSWs is the views of the learners in question. The Code of Practice prioritises the views of the young people and insists that these views should be taken into account. Young people embarking on their post-16 educational pathway may not wish to be singled out as needing additional help in, or out, of the learning environment. However, this help may be crucial to their progress. Here, once again, the negotiation and diplomatic skills of the SENCO must be brought into play. Learners may welcome the support they need. If this is not the case, strategies to ensure that support is given and accepted must be agreed with the young person and the colleague tasked to offer support in any given situation. This must also, of course, be negotiated with the group/subject/session tutor so that a shared and collaborative approach can be taken to support the student.

6.4(iii) Other colleagues within the setting

There are a number of other colleagues with whom the SENCO needs to communicate/work/liaise and these will vary depending on the size and nature of the setting and the manner in which it is organised.

Some settings have dedicated staff who organise and monitor work experience placements. These colleagues may be used to organising the placement of students without additional needs. Should this be the case, the SENCO will need to ensure that, when organising a placement, there is a shared understanding of:

a The nature of the learner's difficulties
b What strategies will support the learner to maintain a successful placement
c What support the learner will need, such as:
  i One-to-one support
  ii Adapted resources, e.g. enlarged instructions for visual impairment
  iii Adapted conditions in terms of environment / equipment
  iv A colleague with knowledge of signing
  v Additional time to complete tasks
  vi Awareness of, for example, autism and how to support the learner
  vii Any safety considerations

If the necessary considerations are not taken into account, the young person may be unable to maintain the placement, leading to lack of self-esteem and a sense of failure.

In a discrete provision for students with learning difficulties/disabilities, it may be expected that any work placement arrangements would be made by a colleague with knowledge and experience of the provision's learners and the support they would need in a work placement – and, indeed, the type of placement which is likely to prove successful. Their knowledge and expertise will prove invaluable if shared with staff members in the mainstream provision who may be required to place students with additional needs. The SENCO is in a key position to facilitate this exchange of information for the benefit of the mainstream learners with particular support requirements.

✓ Action

Ensure that all colleagues with responsibility for arranging work placements take into consideration the needs of the learner (a–c, vii above).

If the establishment is in a position to offer extracurricular activities, the SENCO has a role to play in ensuring that the activity leaders are, as above, informed and prepared to offer the support required by students with learning difficulties/disabilities.

Again, depending on the organisation of the setting, there may be a range of other colleagues, such as welfare officers, refectory staff, technicians or estates/premises staff, who should, as far as is practical, be made aware of the challenges of learners and how they can assist them in their daily educational experience.

✓ Action

Inform all colleagues, including refectory and administrative staff, of the particular needs or requirements in respect of individual learners with specific challenges.

6.5 External and in-house staff development

The need for training and development depends almost entirely on the situation in which each education provider finds itself. The 'almost' is included here as, from time to time, mandatory training must be undertaken, e.g. Safeguarding, or Equality and Diversity. That said, each SENCO must have an overview of the requirements for development in relation to their own colleagues.

The diverse attitudes, experiences and expertise of colleagues has been discussed in section 6.3 and evaluation of these will give an ongoing picture of what is required; but it must never be assumed that once training has taken place the need has been addressed. Staff turnover and student intake have an ongoing impact on the maintenance of skills levels. Equally important is the need to evaluate the impact of the training staff members have received.

Table 6.2 Training and development strategies

Training and development	Associated issues	Benefits	Costs to establishment
Shadowing more experienced colleagues	Timetabling – cover for classes while shadowing	First-hand examples of good practice	Cost of cover, although in practice staff often absorb this time without cost to the establishment
Online packages	Time available for staff to undertake Lack of personal contact No facility for discussion	Many staff can be trained under one package	Cost of online package
Whole-setting/-department development training	May be general rather than specific as time may be limited	Can be targeted to the needs of the staff May be able to be delivered by specialist colleagues within setting	Cost of external specialist, or may be subsumed into staff costs if delivered by staff member
External courses	Time for staff to attend and undertake study	Specialist – targeted Relevant to staff needs Information and knowledge can be disseminated to colleagues	Potentially cost of cover Fees paid by establishment or support with payment of fees

Once again, the ethos of the organisation and its commitment to the support of vulnerable learners cannot be overemphasised in its importance here. Training and development can take place at many levels but there is always a cost involved.

SENCOs need to evaluate the impact of the training on the expansion of knowledge and skills and, most importantly, on the support given to students. Where the impact is considered to be positive, this can inform management decisions regarding further staff development opportunities.

Since 2008, the National Award for SEN Co-ordination has been a statutory award for newly appointed SENCOs in maintained schools and attracts 60 credits at master's level (Level 7). As described in section 6.3, there is, at present, no requirement for SENCOs in post-16 education to undertake this Award although they may wish to do so. The courses leading to the award are offered nationwide and there are, of course, funding implications. It is to be hoped that should FE SENCOs wish to undertake this qualification, their establishment would be supportive of this opportunity in practical and financial ways.

✓ Action

Work closely with the colleagues responsible for organising staff development opportunities to ensure that appropriate training is available for staff and that this is well publicised, including the facility to have one-to-one support if required.

6.6 Colleagues from outside the setting

As discussed in earlier sections, the SENCO is required to work with a range of colleagues within his/her setting. These may be tutors, support staff and/or management team members, not forgetting the other in-house colleagues mentioned above in section 6.5.

However, the SENCO's role is certainly not limited to work that involves internal colleagues. He/she will need to work in close co-operation with his/her own LA as well as with the other LAs from which the setting's learners come. This may involve working with a number of different LAs, each of which may be organised in a different way and have different paperwork and procedures.

In **Chapter 7**, the administration and procedures surrounding the role of the SENCO will be examined and it will become evident that a key partnership is that between the SENCO and the LA. If a collaborative relationship with the LA can be established, this can only facilitate the smooth operation of the support for the learners. Depending on the way in which the LA is organised, it is to be recommended that the FE SENCO develops a good working relationship with a key LA staff member or LA team who are involved with young people with learning difficulties/disabilities. As described in section 6.4(ii), the individual or team may be involved with SEN provision across the range of key stages, some of them even specifically with post-16 provision. Whatever their modus operandi, the benefits of the establishment of this relationship cannot be overstated.

There is a range of external professional specialists with whom the SENCO may need to liaise. In many cases the requirement for their involvement will have been identified via a learner's Education, Health and Care Plan (EHCP), either generated in the local LA or the LA in which the learner was previously located, and previous arrangements will have been made. In the former case, there is scope for them to be continued, albeit at different times/locations. In the latter case, new local arrangements will need to be put in place.

These external colleagues may be speech therapists, diabetes nurses, physiotherapists, social workers or probation officers, to name a few. If an existing local relationship is in place, the SENCO will need to ensure that if the learner is to attend treatment or receive visits in college/learning time, arrangements are made which cause minimum disruption to their timetable. If the young person comes to the setting from a different location/ LA, the SENCO will need to liaise with both LAs to feel confident that appropriate arrangements have been made to continue support. Then, as before, minimum disruption to learning should be co-ordinated.

As mentioned in section 4.1, additional needs are not inevitably identified before the start of post-16 education and this may be for any number of reasons. It is not within the remit of this book to question why this occurs but simply to recognise that this will occasionally be the case. Some disabilities may intensify over time, e.g. an increase in hearing or sight impairment, or progress of a disease. Furthermore, illness or trauma can result in physical, sensory or learning impairment.

For these reasons, it may fall to the SENCO to evaluate the additional support needed by a learner and request assessment for an EHCP (**Chapter** 7) or make arrangements within the setting to support needs.

In the latter case, resources and appropriately qualified staff may be available for deployment. In the former case, the SENCO needs to approach the LA to request an EHCP in order to secure the services of appropriate professionals who can offer specialist support to the learner.

On a practical level, as before, the SENCO needs to facilitate the incorporation of the external professional's visits into the learner's timetable, in collaboration with subject/ group/class tutors.

✓ Action

Establish collaborative relationships with external colleagues who support learners with regard to specific challenges.

✓ Action

Ensure that contact between learners and external colleagues is facilitated, while minimising, as far as possible, disruption to a learner's timetable.

Key points from this chapter:

- The SENCO can play a key role in informing their governing body (GB) and senior management team (SMT) about the importance of supporting learners with learning difficulties/disabilities.
- The SENCO can facilitate training for their GB and SMT to ensure they are aware of their obligations and the training, resources and facilities required to fulfil these.
- Teaching staff vary in terms of their qualifications, training and experience regarding learners with a range of challenges.
- Teaching staff also vary in terms of their attitudes to responsibility for the support of students with additional needs.
- TAs should be managed and directed to support learning.
- There are a range of qualifications available to colleagues, teaching and support staff, including specialist training relating to learning difficulties/disabilities.
- Ongoing training, to raise awareness and increase skills, should be available to all colleagues.

7 Administration and procedures

In this chapter:

7.1 A person-centred approach

The revised SEND Code of Practice 0–25 years (2015) places the pupil/student/young person at the centre of the systems designed to offer them the support required. This is particularly significant in post-16 provision. After compulsory school age – the end of the academic year in which the learner turns 16 – he/she must be the key voice in decision-making. The parents/carers may continue to be involved and support the young person in their decision-making, but he/she has the right to refuse their involvement. Effective working with parents/carers and families is discussed in section 8.2.

The young person's choice of educational setting must be respected and the local authority (LA) is required to comply with this selection and name the establishment chosen on the Education, Health and Care Plan (EHCP), if appropriate (see also section 8.1).

There may be occasions when there is a conflict between the right to name a particular provider and that provider's perception of their ability to meet the needs of the young person. Here, appeals can be made to the First-Tier Tribunal (Special Educational Needs and Disability, Department for Education (DfE), 2014). In cases which do not relate solely to the college which will be named in an EHCP, the young person and their parents, if applicable, must first contact an independent mediation adviser. Should mediation not be required or prove unsuccessful in resolving the conflict, the adviser will issue a certificate, allowing them to proceed with the appeal to the tribunal.

Where a student is dissatisfied with their course or the support they are receiving they should, in the first instance, make informal representation to their tutor or the principal via the college's formal complaints procedure. In a further education (FE) setting, if the complaint remains unresolved the student may take up their case with the Skills Funding Agency (SFA). The procedures for this can be found on the Skills Funding Agency's website. For sixth-form colleges or other Education Funding Agency (EFA) funded providers, the procedure is available on the GOV.UK website.

7.2 Education, Health and Care Plans

By 2018, Statements of Special Educational Needs must be replaced by EHCPs (DfE/ Department of Health, 2015). Some LAs take a gradual approach to this replacement while others have chosen to make the change in one move.

For this reason, there will be a mixture of different systems in place in many colleges and other providers, particularly if the students attending come from a variety of different LAs. By 2018, however, all support plans will take the form of EHCPs so it is useful here to describe what is required at each stage of the Plan.

While there is no statutory format for the EHCP, there is a requirement that it should be a forward-looking document and contain specific sections:

Plans must have sections A to K labelled individually.

Section A	Views, interests and aspirations of the young person
Section B	The young person's special educational needs
Section C	The young person's health needs related to their special educational needs
Section D	The young person's social care requirements in relation to their special educational needs
Section E	The outcomes identified for the young person. Chapter 9 of the Code of Practice (2015) requires that this section should include outcomes for adult life. However, this section should also include the arrangements for setting shorter-term targets.
Section F	The special educational provision required by the young person
Section G	Any health provision reasonably required by the learning difficulties or disabilities which result in the young person having special educational needs
Section H1	Any social care provision which is required to be made for a young person (under 18) in accordance with Section 2 of the Chronically Sick and Disabled Persons Act 1970
Section H2	Any other social care provision reasonably required to support the learning difficulties or disabilities which result in the young person having special educational needs, including any adult social care provided to meet a young person's needs under the Care Act 2014
Section I	The name and type of the post-16 institution or other institution to be attended by the young person
Section J	Where there is a personal budget, the details of how this will support particular outcomes must be given. The special educational needs and outcomes to be met by direct payment must be specified.

Section K Where the young person is in or above Year 9, the EHCP is required to include (in Sections F, G, H1 or H2 as applicable) the provision required to support preparation for adulthood and independent living

(SEND Code of Practice 0–25 years, 2014, 9:62)

✓ Action

Become familiar with the style and format of EHCPs used in the different LAs from which the organisation's learners transfer.

The detail, if any, required in the individual sections of the EHCP will depend on the needs of the young person and will, therefore, be varied. It will fall to the SENCO of the college or other post-16 provision to interpret the needs of individual learners and to manage the arrangements to put the appropriate support in place. If this is undertaken in a robust and meaningful way from the outset, the monitoring of individual goals and the provision of information will be facilitated and result in relevant outcomes.

An EHCP ceases when a young person leaves education to take up employment (excluding apprenticeships) or when he/she enters Higher Education. Similarly the Plan ceases if the young person (aged 18 or over) leaves education and no longer wishes to engage in further training. Although the scope of the Code of Practice extends to the age of 25, it is possible for a Plan to cease before that time if, on review, all the outcomes of the Plan have been achieved.

There are particular circumstances relating to the cessation of EHCPs, and FE SENCOs should be aware of them. The Code of Practice 9.202, 9.203, 9.204 (DfE, 2014; 2015 reviewed) gives details of the statutory duties of the LA in these circumstances, for instance a young person being given a custodial sentence, being excluded or leaving before the end of their course. The maintenance and/or cessation of EHCPs remains the responsibility of the LA. However, it is crucial that education providers and LAs work together to ensure that the best possible provision is secured and, when applicable, its cessation handled appropriately (SEND Code of Practice 0–25 years, Chapter 9).

7.3 Requesting an EHCP assessment

As described in **Chapter 4**, many young people who have high-level support needs will embark on their post-16 phase of education having already been assessed for and in possession of a EHCP (or, until 2018, a Statement of Special Educational Needs). In these cases, the post-16 SENCO will need to work with the young person, colleagues, the LA(s) and outside professionals to ensure that the appropriate support is put in place and is effective in underpinning progress.

There may be occasions, however, when it is considered appropriate for the post-16 setting to request the LA to instigate assessment for an EHCP. This may be the result of a previously undiagnosed difficulty, a trauma leading to a new need or the deterioration of an existing condition. Similarly, a student may have recently moved from overseas or from another part of the United Kingdom. A Statement or Plan from, for instance,

Northern Ireland, Scotland or Wales would not be recognised in England, as each area has its own funding arrangements.

Whatever the background to the situation, there are some key considerations relating to the request for an EHCP assessment, preparation being the most important.

In order to make representation to the LA panel, who will consider the request for an EHCP, the setting must demonstrate that specific additional support, over and above what could be considered to be 'reasonable adjustments', is required by the learner.

The education provider also needs to demonstrate that a graduated approach has been put in place to support the young person's learning and that, over time, this has proven to be insufficient to ensure consistent progress. Here, the college or other provider needs to provide evidence that steps taken to enable the learner to achieve their outcomes/goals have been successful or otherwise and what interventions have/have not been effective.

The provider will need to present evidence of any assessment by EP or other professionals and prove that sufficient time has been allowed for any strategies identified to demonstrate their effectiveness. Evidence that the young person and, where appropriate, their family/ carers have been involved in discussions is also required.

The setting will also be required to demonstrate that collaboration with the LA via the SEN caseworker or other officer has taken and is taking place.

As can be seen, a considerable amount of evidence is necessary to underpin the request for a young person to be granted an EHCP. This will involve a large amount of documentation to support the application. It must, however, be summarised in order that the LA panel, comprising appropriate specialists in a range of different fields, can identify the needs of the young person, their challenges and the support they will need to achieve their future goals. The summary must show:

- any reasonable adjustments necessary have been made and to what extent the needs of the young person extend beyond the scope of these adjustments;
- graduated support strategies have been implemented and the extent to which they were successful/unsuccessful;
- evidence to support the outcomes of any professional assessments;
- a plan for support to be implemented in terms of, for instance, staffing, resources, systems;
- the young person has been at the centre of discussions and planning for their support needs.

In the event of dramatic trauma or accident resulting in additional needs, some of the points above may be considered inapplicable, e.g. previous strategies.

To summarise, then, the education provider must be completely prepared before the meeting at which their application is to be considered. The bringing together of this evidence is time-consuming but, if effectively undertaken, will ensure a speedier outcome for the young person in question.

> ✓ **Action**
>
> Become familiar with the relevant LAs' evidence requirements and their format.

7.3(i) Timings

When deciding to apply for an EHCP assessment, it is worth taking into consideration what is involved with the whole process and the implications for meeting the statutory timescales. If needs have been identified over several months, it might be tempting to seek to ensure that appropriate support can be planned for the next academic year. Bear in mind, however, that, if applying for an assessment towards the end of an academic year, the summer period may not allow sufficient opportunity for the professionals to meet with the young person and share information within the specified time limits.

From application to Week 4

When a request is received, together with supporting documents, the LA will send requests for information from relevant parties within education, health and social care, giving them **four weeks** in which to respond. A multi-agency panel will then discuss the case and decide whether or not to continue to an EHCP assessment. If this is agreed, further evidence will be requested for consideration in **Week 12**.

The LA **must** decide whether or not an assessment is required and this decision must be communicated to the young person within **six weeks** of the receipt of the request.

Week 6

The young person and, if appropriate, their family/carers, as well as all interested parties are advised of the panel's decision. Opportunities to update or confirm reports are offered.

Week 12

All reports, updated as appropriate, must have been received. The LA's Commissioning Officer may liaise with some or all parties to discuss potential provision and planning for the young person. The request will then be presented to the LA's funding panel and decisions made will be communicated accordingly.

Week 13

Where an EHCP has been agreed Service Lead Officers or their delegates will agree resourcing to support the young person. At this stage any amendments to the proposed EHCP may be made.

Week 16

A draft EHCP is issued. The young person and/or their parents/carers, if appropriate, have 15 days to make any further requests and/or comments regarding the Plan.

Week 20

Final EHCP published.

A young person or their parents/carers may disagree with the LA about a decision relating to their EHCP assessment or the EHCP itself. This might be, for instance, a decision not to carry out an assessment, not to issue a Plan, the education provision specified in a Plan or the college specified in it and they can appeal to the First-Tier Tribunal (Special Education Needs and Disability). Before appealing they must first contact an independent mediation adviser unless the dispute is solely regarding the college that will be named on an EHCP. If the disagreement cannot be resolved by mediation, the mediation adviser will issue a certificate allowing them to proceed with their appeal to the Tribunal (DfE, 2014). Full information about complaints, including mediation and appeals, is given in Chapter 11 of the Code of Practice.

Different LAs have different criteria for the consideration of 'reasonable adjustments' and it is important to ensure that there is clarity about these.

✓ Action

Obtain the policy/guidelines on 'reasonable adjustments' for the relevant LA.

7.4 Student Profiles/Individual Learner Records

It is good practice for all learners, with or without learning difficulties/disabilities, to have goals/targets to which they work. This makes tracking of progress more effective and, importantly, offers the learners a clarity of purpose. The nomenclature may vary in different establishments – ILP, ILR, IEP or another term – but the purpose of these records is universal: to set out clearly the steps the learner is to achieve on their journey towards their overall goal.

A Student Profile (SP) describes the student's strengths and areas for development, and any particular circumstances which have a bearing on their learning. In some cases the Profile and Record/Plan will be contained in one document, in others there may be two separate documents. The key requirement is that they are useful and contain meaningful information.

✓ Action

Undertake an audit of learners' plans/records and other documentation for quality assurance purposes.

One might assume that, where a learner has an EHCP this would facilitate the design of the Individual Plan/Record. It is important to remember, however, that the quality of EHCPs is variable and that it may be necessary to 'translate' the outcomes described in Section E into meaningful and measurable short-term goals. A key feature in the long- and short-term goals for learners with learning difficulties/disabilities must include the way in which they are being prepared for adulthood. Realistic targets which will support them to gain employment, live independently, be included in community life and maintain a healthy lifestyle should – if suitable for their needs and aimed at levels appropriate to the individual student – feature as part of the support programme (see also **Chapter 9**).

The Plans/Records relating to learners must, of course, be shared with the academic, vocational and support staff who will be working with the young person. Departmental teaching staff may need support to assist with breaking down learners' curricular goals into steps which are achievable, with or without additional support. These will, naturally, be subject-specific and relate to the curriculum area in question.

Departmental colleagues may additionally require considerable support in the area of social goals and outcomes, and it is here that detail and precision is needed. Where a discrete provision exists, the specialists in this area may be able to share their expertise in setting meaningful and measurable goals.

Where an overall outcome is stated as:

'Student A's goal is to improve social interaction with his/her peers', this should be broken down into steps which are appropriate to that student's needs, and are clear and measurable. For example:

Student A's goals are:

- to greet two group members by name at the start of each session;
- to work collaboratively in a small group when asked;
- to use appropriate language when working with peers.

These are specific and measurable goals and should be given an appropriate time constraint. Clearly, if the student was able to do these things once and once only, this would not demonstrate a newly developed skill. However, if they were able to demonstrate this consistently over a number of sessions/weeks, a new ability can be said to have been acquired.

Similarly, where an overall outcome is stated as:

'Student B's goal is to demonstrate appropriate behaviour in class', the learner's individual challenges should be considered and steps which are meaningful can be agreed. For example:

Student B's goals are:

- to avoid unacceptable language in the session;
- to allow others to listen to the tutor without distraction;
- to ask for help when necessary.

Again, these are specific and measurable and, as in the example above, time constrained; in this way the learner has the opportunity to demonstrate ability, or otherwise, meaning that targets can then be considered achieved or in need of review/additional support

The above are intended to be examples only. The key point is that Plans/Records are as valuable as their content. If targets and goals are vague, they fail to be useful; if they are tight and appropriate, they enable learners and staff to be clear about what is required to achieve and make progress.

Whether or not the learner has an EHCP, regular review is necessary to monitor progress and this should be at relevant and appropriate intervals to offer sufficient time for achievement to have taken place. Where targets have been met, new ones, in keeping with the EHCP and/or Profile/Plan, can be set. Where targets are not consistently met, there may be a need to adjust them, offer additional support or revise them to give the learner a greater opportunity to succeed.

✓ Action

Ensure that long-term goals for learners include those, as individually appropriate, that relate to preparation for adulthood, e.g. employment, independent living, community inclusion and maintaining a healthy lifestyle.

✓ Action

Provide training for colleagues to support the setting of meaningful, achievable and realistic targets.

7.5 Reviewing EHCPs

LAs are required to review EHCPs every 12 months (minimum). These reviews must focus on the progress the learner has made towards the goals set out in the EHCP. Whether or not these outcomes remain appropriate must also be considered. Information must be gathered regarding the special education, health and social care of the young person and its effectiveness. Decisions will be taken with regard to the continuing appropriateness of the EHCP and/or whether any changes should be made or whether the Plan should be discontinued. Where new outcomes are considered necessary, they will be agreed at this stage.

Within four weeks of the review meeting, the LA must decide whether to maintain, amend or cease the EHCP and inform the young person and, where appropriate, their parents/carers. The relevant educational establishment must also be notified (Code of Practice, 9.177).

Implications for post-16 providers

It falls to the SENCO in a post-16 provision to collate the information about students' progress in order to undertake the reviews. This, of course, will require robust communication strategies as a student may be with a number of different staff members during their course.

Perhaps one of the greatest challenges for SENCOs when reviewing EHCPs is timing. A Plan may have been agreed at any point during an academic year and its review is required to take place within 12 months of its commencement. This means that, where a young person's EHCP was agreed in, for instance, October of the previous year, it will be due for review almost immediately after his/her course has started. Inevitably this will mean that information will be required from present and past providers.

✓ Action

Set up a schedule for each learner with an EHCP, giving deadlines and prompts for the collection of information for reviews.

When drawing together information from LAs and other professionals, it is important that this is done in a timely fashion. Some LAs and professionals are reluctant, for reasons of security and confidentiality, to send information electronically, preferring to use postal or fax methods. In both of the latter cases, it is important to ensure that systems are in place for postal or fax communications to be promptly and securely delivered to the appropriate staff member, as delays can affect the ability of the SENCO to ensure the timely review of a learner's Plan.

✓ Action

Ensure that systems for the transfer of information are secure and that they take into account the timescales needed to accommodate the preferred method of delivery for different LAs.

7.6 Liaison and monitoring meetings; providing information

Communication must a key feature of the support for young people with learning difficulties/disabilities as the revised Code of Practice is designed to offer a unified, single approach involving all relevant parties.

There may be numerous people concerned with a young person and all need to make a contribution to monitoring meetings. The learner him/herself is key in this process and must be consulted and involved at each stage. If the student is agreeable, their parents/ carers may also be involved (see sections 8.1 and 8.2). Depending on the learner's needs, a number of other professionals may be required to contribute to the review of progress made under the EHCP.

The challenges of the involvement of a range of different people are largely logistical. The greater the number of contributors, the greater the difficulty in arranging meetings at a mutually convenient time. The professionals involved are busy people and it may be necessary to be creative when arranging the sharing of information. Video conferences, webinars and Skype groups can be alternative methods of communication and discussion when it is not possible to have all parties together in the same location at the same time. While these issues may appear tricky, the important point is that all those involved with the support of a young person are given the opportunity to contribute to the feedback and that information is shared in a timely manner in order to review the progress of the learner and to make any adjustments considered necessary to their progress.

Key points from this chapter:

- The young person should be at the centre of discussions and planning regarding their needs and support.
- Education, Health and Care Plans (EHCP) vary in format, but there are requirements as to what must be included in them.
- Planning and the provision of appropriate evidence are crucial when requesting an assessment for an EHCP.
- While the design and format of Individual Learner Profiles/Records varies between providers, there must be meaningful, measurable, realistic and appropriate goals included in the required monitoring process for learners with, and without, learning difficulties/disabilities.
- There are statutory timescales for reviewing EHCPs. It is crucial, therefore, to establish monitoring and feedback systems to inform this process.
- As information and feedback is drawn from a number of internal and external sources, it is vital to establish and maintain effective communication strategies.
- All relevant parties must be given the opportunity to contribute to learner feedback.
- Ensure that feedback from relevant parties includes that relating to preparation for adult life.
- Given the logistical challenges involved in arranging multi-agency meetings, a range of communication systems should be considered, including the use of technology for conference calling, Skype groups and webinars.

8 Working with families, schools and other professionals

In this chapter:

8.1 Who is involved with decisions about the young person? The voice of the young person

The end of the academic year in which a student turns 16 marks the end of compulsory schooling. From this point the right to make requests and decisions under the Children and Families Act 2014 applies directly to the young person him/herself, rather than to his/her parents/carers. Provided that the young person is in agreement, parents/carers can continue to support them in making decisions or act on their behalf and in the majority of cases they do, in fact, remain closely involved.

This has particular significance for colleges. Where a learner under the age of 18 causes concern in respect of welfare or behaviour, colleges would normally involve the family and, where this is their policy, they should continue to do so. Although the Children and Families Act 2014 gives rights directly to young people from the end of compulsory schooling, this does not require any changes to a college's safeguarding or welfare policies (DoE, 2014).

Where a young person lacks mental capacity (Mental Capacity Act, 2005; Children and Families Act, 2014) their representative, potentially a family member, is empowered to make decisions on their behalf. Annex 1 of the SEND Code of Practice 0–25 years gives further details of the Mental Capacity Act (2005) and how it relates to young people and their parents/carers.

✓ Action

Read Annex 1 of the Code of Practice.

As illustrated in section 7.2, a young person with an Education, Health and Care Plan (EHCP), or their representative (see above), has the opportunity to name a specific establishment at which they wish their education to continue. The local authority (LA) then has a duty to name that institution in the EHCP unless, following consultation with the institution, the LA 'determines that it is unsuitable for the young person's age, ability, aptitude or SEN, or that to place the young person there would be incompatible with efficient use of resources or the efficient education of others' (Code of Practice, 7.3). Should the establishment be named in an EHCP, the post-16 provision in question then has a duty to admit the young person and to plan appropriate provision for them.

As is evident here, the wishes of the young person are considered central and LAs or providers who fail to follow these statutory requirements open themselves to appeal under the Equality Act 2010. An outline of the young person's right to appeal against issues relating to their EHCP is given in section 7.3i. No establishment, or LA, wishes to become involved in disputes and/or appeals if these can be avoided. It is therefore important that providers and LAs work closely together on the matter of admissions, and that where it is considered there are grounds for refusal, evidence to support this decision is robust.

It is, then, vital that students have the opportunity to express their views, wishes and concerns and that, where necessary, they are given appropriate support to do so. This is particularly important when discussing the support planned for them. For instance, it may be deemed appropriate that a student receives one-to-one support in some or all sessions. This may, however, be a type of support that is unwelcome to the student as he/she feels singled out by it. Should this be the case, a discussion **with the student** is required to establish the way forward in terms of support. Some learners dislike being removed from the main session for small group work as, again, they feel picked out in some way, while others relish the opportunity to focus in a smaller, quieter environment for part of a session. These examples illustrate the necessity to engage the student in meaningful discussion about their support and how it might be undertaken. There may be a need for compromise but if the learner is involved with the conversation, they will feel that systems are being put in place with them rather than being imposed on them.

In the same way, when it is time to review progress the student should have the opportunity to offer their views on their development, the support they receive and its effectiveness or otherwise, and how they feel this should be maintained or amended. Learners, with or without EHCPs, should be part of an ongoing monitoring and review system and the Code of Practice places a high priority on their views. As discussed, there may be a divergence between the type of support offered by the provider and that with which the learner feels comfortable. Many young people prefer not to receive attention which singles them out from their peers and there may be a need for negotiation and diplomacy on the part of the SENCO regarding the design and implementation of effective support systems.

> ✓ **Action**
>
> At the planning and review stages engage in discussion with learners to establish how they feel about different support methods.

At this stage of young adulthood, some young people who have embarked on a post-16 education pathway may feel that the need to involve their families/carers, as they were required to do when at school, is no longer necessary.

8.2 Working with families/carers

It has been established that once young people embark on their post-16 education career, they are not obliged to involve their family/carers in decisions and discussions if they do not wish to do so unless, as described in section 8.1, their mental incapacity to make independent decisions is proven.

In the vast majority of cases, however, learners are happy for their family/carers to continue to be involved and to support them with their progress. Where this is the case, a collaborative relationship may be fostered to provide a consistent approach to the support of the young person, whether or not he/she has an EHCP. A robust communication system is key to the success of this relationship and this, depending on circumstances and geography, can take many forms – for example, face-to-face meetings, telephone conversations or email.

If families/carers are aware of the strategies in place in the education setting, they may be able to mirror these in the home environment, reinforcing the support for the young person.

> ✓ **Action**
>
> Use best endeavours to establish mutually communicative relationships with families/carers.

There are circumstances, however, where it is more difficult to develop this mutually supportive approach and there may be a number of reasons for this. In some cases, the parent(s)/carers may themselves have a learning difficulty or have major gaps in their own education. Here, it is important that their involvement is seen to be valued and strategies devised to empower them to give what support they are able to offer. If the family/carers have a learning need of their own, they will be able to identify only too well with the young person's difficulty and feelings, placing them in a strong position to offer support and encouragement. Any academic weakness should not be allowed to make them feel inferior and the provider may need to develop systems of communication – for instance verbal rather than written – in order to enlist support, inform and discuss.

Some parents/carers may be what Feiler (2010) describes as 'hard to reach' and, again, this may have its basis in a range of different circumstances. Often an unhappy educational experience in the individual's own past leads to suspicion of schools/colleges and a reluctance to engage with the system. Here, while being supportive of the young person, the parent/carer may find it difficult to visit the setting and/or enter into discussions with the professionals. It is important that recognition of their situation is given and it is the provider's role to continue to seek to engage the family. Avoiding overly formal situations which may be intimidating to some carers and using regular, less formal conversations may gradually draw the family into a supportive relationship. The learner can only benefit from greater involvement and, as a bonus, the carers' view of the education system may be revised into a more positive one.

While some parents/carers, as above, may wish to remain aloof from the educational setting, others may fail to recognise the particular difficulties experienced by the young person in question. If an EHCP is in place, the likelihood is that the family is aware of the extent of the learner's challenges. However, some young people who have a learning difficulty, but are not in possession of an EHCP, may find themselves in a different

Table 8.1 Parent/carer involvement

Involvement	**Circumstances**	**Approach**
Involved and supportive Recognise the need for support for the young person	Able to respond to discussions with education provider and to engage in mutually supportive strategies Able to offer support outside college to further progress	Discuss strategies and how these can be reinforced Ongoing information and feedback
Involved and supportive Recognise the need for support for the young person	May lack the capacity to offer academic support May have some needs themselves	Ensure support is valued Consider alternative methods of communication Tailor requests and information to the needs of the family/carers
Disengaged with the system May wish the system to take over without input from themselves May not recognise the needs of the young person	Perhaps had a bad educational experience themselves Overloaded and feel unable to cope with further stresses Unable to accept that the young person has a particular difficulty	Ongoing attempts to engage Supportive approach Sensitive discussion and requests for support Diplomatic management of aspirations

position. They will have struggled with some, or all, aspects of school life. Some families may feel that this has been the fault of the school rather than any condition affecting their child/charge. Where this is the case, there are challenges for the education provider. First, tact and diplomacy are required to explain the nature of the difficulties the young person is experiencing and how these are to be addressed. Additionally, and again requiring a high level of interpersonal skills, it may be necessary to manage unrealistic aspirations on the part of the family.

✓ Action

Become familiar with the circumstances of families/carers in order to offer a range of different methods of communication and support.

8.3 Liaison with schools

Here the term 'schools' can be taken to include any previous education provider, for example a previous post-16 provider from which a learner has transferred.

When a young person with an EHCP is admitted to a post-16 education setting, a considerable amount of information will be available in the Plan. This will include, as described in section 7.2, the goals, challenges and circumstances of the new student. This, in turn, will inform planning for teaching and for support.

Many learners with learning difficulties/disabilities, however, will embark on their post-16 phase of education without an EHCP. While there is an argument that promotes a fresh, no-baggage start in a new setting with a clean slate, there is a stronger argument which welcomes as much information as it is possible to receive. Of course, learners may respond differently to a new environment but the new setting should seek to glean as much sound, informed detail as possible from previous providers. Educational background, challenges and details of difficulties are invaluable when planning support for new learners, together with information on the strategies that have, and have not, proved to be successful in the past. As in section 8.1, it is essential that the learner is involved in discussion about their needs, as they will have valuable contributions to offer regarding their previous experiences and the success, or otherwise, of the support they received.

Pupils in secondary schools should be preparing for transition from, at the latest, the start of Year 9 (Code of Practice, 9.63; 9.68), although some would argue that onward planning should start at the beginning of each educational setting. Colleges and other post-16 providers should, where possible, liaise with the previous settings of potential students well in advance of the enrolment stage. In this way, the suitability of the course(s), the challenges faced by individual learners, reasonable adjustments which may be required and the support they will need to have in place can be discussed and planned. This is, of course, logistically more straightforward where potential students are in the same geographical area as the post-16 provider.

Where the setting offers both mainstream and discrete provision for learners with learning difficulties/disabilities, the SENCO may be able to draw on the expertise of specialist staff when assessing the needs of potential students. Where the provision is mainstream only, the SENCO, or a delegated colleague, will need to manage the recruitment process according to the specific needs that are identified in the applications of potential students.

Setting with mainstream and discrete provision for students with learning difficulties/disabilities

- Staff with responsibility for recruitment liaise with local school/education providers; this may be in the form of visits to schools, recruitment fairs, visits to college, link days/weeks
  - Mainstream and specialist staff work together to identify appropriate provision and support required by individual learners
  - Liaison with SENCO (if not part of recruitment team) takes place to establish needs and facilitate planning
  - Additional information from schools/previous providers is requested to ensure comprehensive view available
- Where initial assessment or on-course feedback indicates additional needs
  - Specialist in-house colleagues are consulted to establish level/type of need and support required
  - Additional information is requested from schools/previous providers

Setting with mainstream provision only

- Staff with responsibility for recruitment liaise with local school/education providers; this may be in the form of visits to schools, recruitment fairs, visits to college, link days/weeks
  - Staff notify SENCO of any potential students who may have additional needs
  - SENCO assesses type and level of support which will be required, seeking specialist advice if required, e.g. from LA, specialist providers
  - SENCO requests additional information from schools/previous providers to ensure comprehensive view available, including support previously in place, etc.
  - SENCO considers preliminary plans regarding funding implications, e.g. adjustments, additional staff, staff training, equipment/resources
- Where initial assessment or on-course feedback indicates additional needs
  - SENCO has discussions with teaching staff to establish nature/level of need
  - If required, SENCO seeks advice from specialist advisers, for instance LA, specialist providers
  - SENCO requests additional information from schools/previous providers
  - SENCO considers financial implications in terms of adjustments, additional staff, staff training, equipment/resources

✓ Action

Actively seek additional information from schools or previous providers as required.

✓ **Action**

Discuss previous support strategies with the learner to establish their feelings about this and the extent to which they found it helpful.

When students are recruited from other geographical areas, it may be more difficult to liaise in person with the young people themselves and with the educational setting previously attended. Modern technology can, however, facilitate the exchange of information in order to establish a full picture of the young person, their needs and the strategies which have, or have not, been successful in their support in the past.

SENCOs will find that, as with EHCPs from different LAs, the quality of the information received from different schools, even within the same LA, may vary considerably.

8.4 Liaison with external professionals

The revised Code of Practice (2015) has, as perhaps its strongest requirement, the ethos of a cohesive team approach to the support of young people with learning difficulties/ disabilities, with the young person placed firmly in the centre of the events. This unified style of working is intended to offer a holistic package, avoid duplication and enhance communication. This is turn, should facilitate the efficient delegation of resources and ensure that all parties involved are able to receive timely information and monitor progress.

Some post-16 learners will have an EHCP and, where this is the case, the Plan will indicate the range of professionals involved in supporting the young person. Many learners with learning difficulties/disabilities will not have an EHCP but will require support or intervention from professionals outside their education setting. The range of parties involved with a young person varies in accordance with the challenges he/she faces.

8.4(i) Local authorities

Whatever the range of professionals engaged with the learners, the LA is the organisation with which it is vital to establish a robust relationship. In the same way that colleges and other post-16 education providers are differently organised to reflect their purpose, size and circumstances, LAs also vary in staffing levels and delegation of responsibilities.

LAs have, for many years, been involved in the support of pupils with special educational needs (SEN) in schools and have, therefore, considerable experience and expertise in this field. Many have teams of specialist advisory teachers, others have access to specially skilled consultants – some have a combination of both. Some LAs are able to offer support with transport for young people with learning difficulties/disabilities while others are not. Size and geography have influences here as, for instance, transport in a large rural LA poses different challenges to transport in a small, unitary LA.

The SENCO should, therefore, establish a professional relationship with the LA Officer who has overall responsibility for the oversight of special educational needs. They in turn may delegate the operation of this relationship to a colleague who is responsible for the post-16 sector, an area which until recently did not fall within the remit of LAs. The size of the LA team relating to post-16 learners will vary depending on the size of the LA and its make-up. Whatever the organisation of the LA, it is in the best interests of the setting, and therefore of the learners, that a working, communicative relationship is established between the SENCO and the relevant officers in the LA.

✓ Action

Establish a robust and collaborative relationship with the relevant LA officer/team.

✓ Action

Make contact with other LAs from which learners may attend the setting, ensuring that a relationship is established with a key officer/team.

Learners with an EHCP

The LA is required by the Code of Practice, (2015) to review EHCPs every 12 months (minimum) and will, therefore, require feedback from providers at timely intervals. Information on progress towards goals will be needed in order to facilitate the maintenance, amendment or, indeed, cessation of a Plan.

In order to meet the timescales involved with the review of EHCPs, the SENCO needs to have a monitoring and feedback system in place so that the colleagues working with a particular young person are able to provide information on progress in advance of the call for review paperwork.

✓ Action

When setting up and maintaining the schedule for reviews (section 7.5), incorporate the possibility of short timescales. This could be because a review is required immediately or soon after a learner starts the course or due to college holidays when the student is not present.

Learners without an EHCP

Many learners with learning difficulties/disabilities do not have or require an EHCP. However, their needs must be addressed and, for the most part, this should be undertaken via high-quality, well-differentiated teaching, adapted resources and additional support.

In settings which include both mainstream and specialist provision, there is scope for the sharing of expertise to extend the skills of mainstream colleagues in their ability to support particular needs. One-to-one support may be available here, if appropriate, as well as a range of other support strategies.

The LA should be in a position to offer advice and contact information where there is a lack of specialism or experience in-house. They may be able to suggest sources of support for particular circumstances, including contacts in specialist provisions who may be able to offer training, support or services. If, for instance, the post-16 setting feels that a young person would benefit from independent travel training, this may not be available within existing staff/budget resources. It may be a need that was not evident when the young person attended school or another educational setting. The LA may be able to offer information about local organisations able to provide this training. Similarly, where particular adaptations/resources are required for a given circumstance, the LA should be in a position to indicate schools/providers who may be able to share expertise. The SENCO should, of course, be aware at all times of the potential cost implications.

8.4(ii) Education, health and care professionals

As described previously, the range of professionals with whom the post-16 SENCO is required to engage is as varied as the range of learners in their charge. Where an EHCP is in place, it is evident who these professionals may be. It is important to remember, however, that learners who do not have an EHCP may also benefit from the input of other agencies.

Where a young person has an EHCP the post-16 SENCO is required to communicate with the other professionals involved in order to ensure that the support for the learners is cohesive and informed. When the LA is required to review an EHCP they will request information from all parties involved in order to undertake a holistic review of the young person's progress and the SENCO should be aware of the timescales involved with regard to each individual learner with an EHCP (see section 7.5).

The annual review must not, of course be the only liaison point between all the professionals involved and ongoing communication between all parties concerned with a young person, with or without an EHCP, is important to the support offered. Colleagues within the setting and in other organisations are busy people and time is a precious commodity. It is important, therefore, to establish and maintain good communication strategies so that information and updates can be exchanged between all those involved with a particular young person.

✓ Action

Draw up a list of the relevant external colleagues involved with each young person, as appropriate, giving contact details, availability and so on, and ensure that communication strategies are in place to maintain effective information exchange.

Who, then, might these external agencies include?

- social services
- educational psychology services
- independent travel advisers
- youth offending services

- probation services
- mental health professionals
- medical professionals, including:
  - diabetes nurses
  - genetic specialists
  - nurse specialising in support for life-limiting conditions
  - general practitioners
  - mental health services, including CAMHS
  - dieticians
  - therapeutic services

Here, the SENCO's role has two elements. First, where a young person already benefits from the input of outside professionals, the SENCO needs to establish a relationship with the key personnel and maintain this in a communicative and informative way, so that a system is established through which each party is aware of developments.

Second, a requirement for input from a particular professional service may arise. This could be due to the identification of a need, the deterioration of an existing condition or a change in circumstances. In this case, it may be necessary to consult specialist colleagues, the LA or other providers to ensure that the appropriate professionals are involved.

Some learner involvement with external professionals will take place outside college time. Where this is the case, robust communication systems are crucial so that both the provider and their external colleagues are able to exchange information and remain up to date. Again, the SENCO needs to ensure that strategies are in place to facilitate this communication.

There may be instances, however, when interaction between young people and external agencies must take place within college time and this requires careful co-ordination on the part of the SENCO. Speech therapy sessions or training in the use of specialist software packages, for example, should be arranged to cause minimum disruption to the timetable of the learner. Equally, independent travel training needs to be organised to coincide with the location in which the learner will spend the rest of their day. The challenges for the SENCO in these circumstances will be the availability of external colleagues and the logistics regarding individual learners' timetables.

✓ Action

Where it is necessary for a young person to see an external specialist during college time, facilitate arrangements that will cause minimum disruption to the learner's timetable.

There may be occasions on which social workers, for example, wish to visit a young person during their learning day. This may be for any number of reasons and, in the interests of the learner's holistic support, this should be facilitated if at all possible. Again it is the responsibility of the SENCO to ensure that this takes place in a supportive atmosphere, but with minimum disruption to the young person's learning.

✓ Action

When there is a requirement for a young person to meet an external colleague during the working day, ensure that there is a suitable, stress-free environment in which the meeting can take place.

Key points from this chapter:

- Young people must be at the centre of discussions and decisions about their support unless, under the Mental Capacity Act, they are shown to lack capacity for this.
- Young people over the age of 16 may decide that their parents/carers should not be involved in their education and decisions surrounding it.
- For a variety of reasons, the degree to which parents/carers are able to engage in the support of young people's education varies.
- It is important to establish a range of different communication strategies to meet the needs of parents/carers.
- The quantity and quality of information received from schools/previous education providers is varied.
- Every effort should be made to acquire as much information from schools/ previous providers as possible.
- Robust strategies must be established for communication with external colleagues who are involved with young people.
- Where it is necessary for learners to meet with external colleagues during learning time, efforts should be made to cause minimum disruption to their timetable and to ensure that meetings take place in appropriate environments.

9 Planning for transition

In this chapter:

9.1 Onward transition; planning from the start

As described in section 8.3, young people should receive support for post-16 transition starting, at the latest, in Year 9 of their secondary education (SEND Code of Practice 0–25 years, 9.63; 9.68). Many would argue that planning for transition should, in fact, feature from the start of each educational phase in order that appropriate goals can be set to develop the skills and understanding required for the next step.

Similarly, it is appropriate to start planning for onward transition at, or before, the start of a learner's further education (FE) experience. This is significant, whether or not a learner has an Education, Health and Care Plan (EHCP), in the design of support arrangements which will be required while working towards outcomes and goals.

The revised Code of Practice (2015) places the wishes and opinions of the young person at its core so it is crucial that informed discussions regarding choices and aspirations take place in a timely fashion (see also sections 8.1 and 8.2).

✓ Action

Discuss long-term aspirations and goals with learners either before or at the start of their courses.

There may be occasions on which the SENCO is required to engage in diplomatic negotiation with learners and/or their families/carers where it is considered that aspirations are unrealistic or, in some cases, insufficiently challenging. While these situations may be difficult, it is important that issues are resolved early. If this does not happen, a young person may face disappointment and loss of self-esteem in the future or fail to achieve their true potential.

As a result of information from schools/previous providers and discussions with new learners, a simple, one-page profile can be drawn up. This should contain not only long-term goals but also what the learner considers to be his/her strengths/challenges, what he/she enjoys and what support he/she has found useful in the past.

✓ Action

Draw up a one-page profile that gives details of aspirations and goals, along with the learner's own views of him/herself and the support he/she needs.

Where an EHCP is in place, overall goals will be stated in the Plan, but the post-16 education provider should, as part of the ongoing monitoring and review process, keep these in mind in order to check progress towards them and/or consider recommending their revision. Where there is no Plan, goals and progress should, of course, be a built-in feature of the planning and monitoring system.

✓ Action

Keep overall goals in mind throughout the monitoring of progress. In order to facilitate this, ongoing feedback from teaching and support colleagues will be required.

9.1(i) Pathways to employment

'The vast majority of young people with SEN are capable of sustainable paid employment with the right preparation and support. All professionals working with them should share this presumption' (Department for Education (DfE), 2014).

The DfE's requirement applies to young people on vocational, academic and discrete provision courses. It is therefore incumbent on providers to identify the skills that are valued by employers and to support learners in acquiring them, be they vocational skills or the personal skills required for successful employment.

The SENCO, in order to have oversight of a young person's progress towards their employability goals, will need to receive regular and meaningful feedback from vocational tutors, personal tutors and any support staff working with him/her. These colleagues work closely with the learners and, for the purpose of receiving feedback, the SENCO requires a robust system to ensure that ongoing monitoring of progress can take place.

Where a young person takes part in work experience (section 9.2), valuable feedback from the placement may contribute to the overall picture of progress.

The ways in which post-16 education provision is designed are numerous and, therefore, so are the systems in place for offering careers advice and assisting young people to find employment. Larger establishments may have a dedicated team of colleagues tasked with this aspect of transition. For other providers, these arrangements may be overseen by a staff member as a part of another role. However the advice and assistance is organised, the SENCO must ensure that there is a knowledge and understanding of the needs of learners with learning difficulties/disabilities and the support that they will need for their transition to employment. This may involve additional support in interview preparation, or at interviews themselves. It may require additional training for travelling to a new location, adapting to a new time routine or managing medication independently. There may be a need for discussion with potential employers regarding, for instance, a hearing impairment or communication difficulty.

✓ Action

If necessary, arrange for the design of bespoke training sessions for learners to assist them with interview techniques; include role play and simulation within the training.

✓ Action

Ensure that colleagues responsible for advising on/facilitating employment opportunities are fully conversant with the needs of individual learners.

✓ Action

With appropriate colleagues, design strategies to ensure that potential employers are informed and aware of any challenges experienced by learners.

Many employers, large and small, welcome applications from young people with learning difficulties/disabilities. The SENCO, and/or whoever takes responsibility for the practical arrangements through which young people may gain employment, will find it useful to compile a 'bank' of local firms and organisations. Clearly, the number and nature of these will vary in accordance with the locality and make-up of the regional community: for instance, the preparation regarding access and travel will depend on local circumstances.

✓ Action

Build up a bank of employers. Include travel considerations, access arrangements and any other details which are relevant to the potential employment of young people with learning difficulties/disabilities.

9.1(ii) Independent living

For some young people with learning difficulties/disabilities, an overall goal may be to live more independently as an adult. This does not mean that they may not also have aspirations to gain employment. For these learners, however, a primary goal is accumulation of the life skills needed to operate outside the family/carer home. Many of the young people in this situation will have an EHCP giving details of the areas of need and what support is likely to be required. Outside agencies, social services/health professionals may be involved with these learners and there is, therefore, a need for discussion and collaboration when considering the next steps.

The skills required to enable the young person to live more independently will be identified by the EHCP or via initial assessment and/or information received from previous providers. Progress towards the acquisition of these skills will have been monitored via the systems in place and recorded on the learner's records. As a result, it should be possible to engage with any other agencies, and/or the young person's family/carers to ensure that support is put in place for transition.

✓ Action

Engage, at an early stage, in discussions with family/carers and other relevant agencies/professionals to secure appropriate arrangements are made for smooth transfer into independent/supported living.

Some learners will leave education and, at this point, if they have an EHCP, this will cease. Others may remain in education but move to more independent living arrangements, supported or unsupported. For some, education will continue in the same or a different setting and preparation work for greater independence in the future will continue. Liaison with others involved with an individual young person is of high importance in order to review and, if necessary, suggest amendments to the support available.

9.1(iii) Further study and training

Some young people may transfer to a different educational organisation. The reasons for this are numerous. It may be considered that more targeted vocational provision is appropriate. Alternatively, if the benefits of specialist provision have been identified, some young people will relocate to a different area.

In section 8.3, the value of sharing information was described and this should be a reciprocal arrangement. Just as the provider welcomes and values the information received from previous settings and other agencies, the organisation to which a learner is bound will find any records and feedback of great value when planning their own support for the young person. Details of the strategies which have proved successful, or otherwise, in the past are key pieces of information when designing a support package for an individual learner.

✓ **Action**

Supply relevant information, including support given and progress made, to the new provider.

9.2 Work experience

Many post-16 education providers are able to offer learners the opportunity to undertake a work experience placement and there is every reason for young people with learning difficulties/disabilities to be included in this.

Work experience placement systems can be organised in a number of different ways and these will depend on the curriculum, the co-operation of local employers and the needs of the students.

Some placements take place in a one- or two-week block. In other circumstances, a regular weekly placement, typically one day a week, may occur throughout the year. While many learners attend their work experience independently, others may need additional support for part, or all, of the placement.

In some organisations, a colleague or several colleagues will have the task of finding, arranging and monitoring all the students undertaking work experience placements. In others, departmental, vocational staff or personal tutors may have this responsibility. In some cases, a designated staff member may be tasked with the organisation of work experience specifically for learners with learning difficulties/disabilities. However the system is arranged, the SENCO, with responsibility for the oversight of the support for students with particular needs, must retain the overview for these arrangements, receive regular feedback and negotiate any additional budgetary requirements. The latter may be related to support staff for some, or all, of a work experience placement or independent travel training in respect of a new location.

✓ **Action**

When placements are suggested or planned, give consideration to any budgetary implications, e.g. support while on placement.

✓ **Action**

According to the arrangements in place for finding and monitoring work placements, ensure that there is a robust feedback system to inform learners' progress records.

9.3 Employment and/or independent living; plans for students' onwards destinations

Whatever the onward destination of a young person – further study, employment, independent living or training – it is important that plans are developed at the appropriate point. Communication is a key issue here and, where there is an EHCP in place, a team of interested parties will make contributions to this.

Many young people with learning difficulties/disabilities do not have an EHCP and it is equally important that their smooth transition is facilitated.

9.3(i) Liaison with providers

If a learner is to transfer to another education/training provider, the sharing of information and records will enable the new setting to assess his/her needs and plan any support required effectively. Details of strategies previously employed and their level of success, or otherwise, will facilitate the co-ordination of fresh support systems. The young person should, again, be at the centre of this planning process and they are more likely to feel confident about their next step if they know that information has been shared. If possible, liaison with the new setting should take place before visits, link events and so on take place, in order to ensure that appropriate care is available for a vulnerable visitor.

9.3(ii) Exploration of appropriate support

There may be a need, as part of the preparation for transition, to explore additional support available. If a young person is, for instance, to travel to a new location for education, employment or training, their ability to travel there may be an issue. It should be part of the planning process to ensure that the learner feels confident in his/her travel arrangements, via travel training, support worker(s), family members or other means. Depending on the needs of the young person, this may be put into effect some time before transition actually takes place or at transition with the support of the new setting. It is important, whatever the timescale, that the SENCO ensures the appropriate arrangements are in place.

The practical steps required to make support plans for this may, depending on the make-up of the provider/college's organisation, be undertaken by colleagues but it is important that, if systems are delegated, the SENCO has oversight of the arrangements and can feel confident that all appropriate communication, liaison and planning has taken place.

Consideration should also be given to the fact that a young person's EHCP will cease when they leave education. If, therefore, a learner with an EHCP is moving into employment, funding for additional support will not be available through the channels previously used.

✓ Action

Ensure that support arrangements are put in place, as required, in advance of transition.

9.3(iii) Exploration of funding available

For some young people with learning difficulties/disabilities there may be funding available for certain types of support through voluntary and charitable organisations. This is often to be found locally and SENCOs may find it useful to develop and maintain a bank of contacts in their own area who may be able to contribute in practical or monetary terms and offer advice regarding further sources of support, specialised training and so on.

✓ Action

Build up a bank of local charities, voluntary organisations and so on, who may be able to support young people in the local community.

Key points from this chapter:

- Plans for onward transition should be a feature of planning from the start of the learner's experience in the setting.
- A one-page profile, drawn up with the young person, will facilitate planning for the future.
- Ongoing feedback from colleagues is essential to inform progress toward future plans.
- Colleagues who offer employment advice must be informed and conversant with the strengths and challenges of individual learners.
- Potential employers should be made aware of the strengths and challenges of individual learners.
- Bespoke training on, for instance, interview skills, should be made available.
- Where learners are likely to transfer to independent or supported living, liaison with appropriate parties should take place well in advance of the transfer.
- Where young people are to move to different educational settings, full information should be supplied in a timely fashion.
- Where work experience is a feature, colleagues arranging this and placement providers must be informed of the needs of the learners.
- Providing additional support at a work placement may involve budgetary considerations.
- It is useful to explore sources of external support available via charities and voluntary organisations.

10 Conclusion

It is apparent, then, that the role of the SENCO in the post-16 education sector is not only an extremely important one but also multi-faceted. The SENCO must have oversight of the support provided for young people with learning difficulties/disabilities and of ensuring that this support is effective. The revised SEND Code of Practice 0–25 years (2014) places the learner firmly at the centre of discussions and decisions regarding their support, and providers and LAs must have regard for this, unless lack of mental capacity has been proven.

The extent to which the responsibilities attached to the SENCO's role are delegated depends on the character, size and location of the organisation concerned. In some cases, the SENCO is involved with all aspects of the role's practicalities, in others some of the functional tasks will be delegated to colleagues. The latter case requires clarity regarding responsibilities and robust communication strategies.

However the provision is organised, the SENCO retains the key role in ensuring that the support for learners with additional needs remains a priority in the setting's planning and delivery. This requires working closely with management to inform, plan and budget. While it is to be hoped that the management's support for systems and resources for learners with learning difficulties/disabilities is not based solely on legislation, it is a key part of the SENCO's role to make sure that they are fully aware of the legal requirements regarding these learners.

The revised Code of Practice (2014) has its base in various legislative requirements and it is important that the SENCO is not only familiar with the relevant legislation but also with the implications this now has for post-16 education providers. There are statutory duties placed on LAs and the SENCO must work closely with the appropriate LA(s) and refer to the local offer published by the authority.

It is expected that post-16 education provision for learners with learning difficulties/disabilities will maintain high expectations and provide appropriate support to promote good outcomes for them as they prepare for adulthood. In order to ensure that support is appropriate and relevant, the SENCO should become familiar with the broad categories of high-incidence difficulties/disabilities, their implications and the knowledge and skills needed to support them. In order for the support to be implemented, it is necessary to become familiar with the existing expertise among colleagues and arrange training if required. This training and development can take a number of different forms, ranging from courses, shadowing colleagues, development days, external trainers and liaison with specialist providers/colleagues. It is suggested that it is good practice to invite the governors and management to become involved with this training as this will raise awareness of the issues involved in the support provided for learners with learning difficulties/disabilities.

Information regarding new students may be supplied by schools and/or previous providers but this will vary in quantity and quality. Robust assessment strategies are required, therefore, in order to identify learners' needs and to plan support; the use of a combination of different assessment methods is helpful in gaining a holistic view of learners' needs. For specific learning difficulties, an appropriately qualified assessor is required, but assessment should not be considered to be a one-off procedure; monitoring must be ongoing in order to recognise previously unidentified difficulties and/or those which develop over time.

As needs are identified, the SENCO must ensure that all reasonable adjustments are in place together with the resources needed to support learners, including support staff. There is a range of different terms and methods of deployment used to describe support staff. Again, providers needs in this respect vary depending on the size and make-up of the existing staff complement, and the knowledge and skills already in place. Careful deployment of staff must be arranged and, as needs arise, additional staff may need to be recruited. As with teaching colleagues, existing experience and knowledge should be audited and appropriate training given where needed. Staff knowledge and skills should be audited regularly to accommodate new colleagues and the current cohort of learners. Close liaison with any medical specialists or other external professionals involved with individual students is needed to provide continuity and consistency.

Teaching colleagues vary in terms of their attitudes, qualifications, training and experience in the support of young people with learning difficulties/disabilities. They must, however, accept that it is part of their role to include learners with additional needs. In fact, highly differentiated teaching is the most appropriate method to support all learners and is considered by OfSTED to be good practice. In some cases, specifically skilled support staff may be required to assist in some or all sessions and, once deployed, these colleagues should work under the direction of the group/subject tutor. Once again, training for teaching colleagues in a variety of forms should be made available in order for them to acquire knowledge, understanding and appropriate skills.

There are a number of procedural aspects required by the revised Code of Practice and, unlike its predecessors, the Code requires that they are followed by establishments providing education and training for young people aged between 16 and 25. Before the revised Code, Statements of Special Educational Needs ended when a pupil reached the age of 16 or left school. Statements are now replaced by Education, Health and Care Plans (EHCPs), which may extend until the young person reaches the age of 25, or may terminate before that time.

Although the format of EHCPs varies between LAs, there are requirements as to their content. There are also statutory timescales for the review of EHCPs. As a result, it is vital to establish and maintain effective communication systems to inform reviews – especially as information may be required not only from colleagues but also from external agencies and professionals – and all relevant parties must be given the opportunity to contribute. In order to overcome the logistics of multi-agency meetings, a range of communication strategies should be considered. Colleges and other post-16 education providers may ask the LA to undertake an assessment for an EHCP and, again, there are strict time constraints on this process. For such an assessment, detailed information is required, so careful and timely preparation is crucial.

At some stage – after one, two or three years – a young person will be ready to move on to the next stage of their early adulthood. The preparation for this should, however, be a feature of planning from the start of the learner's experience in the setting. Just as information received from previous providers is useful when students join the setting, this should be available to the next experience in which the young person is to engage – employment, voluntary work, independent living or further training/education.

In many settings, work experience is a feature. Where this is the case, the SENCO should ensure that those tasked with arrangements for this are fully aware of the needs of the individual learners and that work placements are prepared and have the ability to accommodate these.

Similarly, where young people are preparing to move into employment, potential employers should be made aware of the abilities and challenges of the applicant. In some cases, bespoke training may be required by students. Interview skills training may be delivered in the setting, while independent travel training may need to be sourced outside and individual LAs should be able to advise as to the availability of this.

As the learners move onto their next stage of adulthood, the SENCO should feel satisfied with the support, encouragement and opportunities they have offered to the young people with learning difficulties/disabilities within their organisation. The SENCO role is not an easy one, nor should it be – it is challenging and, for those working in post-16 provision, potentially a steep learning curve.

The SENCO, then, must be a learner, teacher/trainer, colleague, communicator, organiser, monitor, mentor, intermediary, negotiator, diplomat, advocate – no pressure then!

Those who take on this challenging, demanding but immensely rewarding role should be recognised and valued for the great contribution they make to the support of the most vulnerable young people in the education community. It is to be hoped that they, rightly, feel proud of the difference they make to the experiences of so many young people, and are aware of the gratitude that is felt towards them by all those who benefit from, or witness the benefits of, their hard work.

Summary of action points

Chapter 1: The changing face of special education

Ensure that, within the organisation, there is clarity regarding overall responsibility for oversight of SEN provision and that management and colleagues are clear about this and about the role they play in the system.

Become familiar with the legislative requirements that relate to your own setting. In particular Chapter 7 of the revised Code of Practice, which refers to young people in education over the age of 16.

Check the progress of the transfers from Statements of Special Educational Needs to EHCPs in the relevant LA(s).

Ensure that there is clarity at all levels regarding who is the staff member with oversight of SEN provision and, where there is delegation, that there are clear lines of communication and responsibilities.

Chapter 2: The Special Educational Needs and Disability (SEND) Code of Practice 0–25 years

Ensure that there is clarity regarding the different categories of commonly occurring learning difficulties and disabilities so that this can be disseminated to colleagues within the organisation.

Draw up a clear table of responsibilities, detailing the statutory responsibilities on the part of the LA and those to be undertaken by the education provider.

Become familiar with the local offer of the LA (and any others from which students attend) and highlight the areas of particular relevance to their own establishment.

Read Chapter 4 of the Code of Practice and highlight the points which are relevant to post-16 provision and to the SENCO's own organisation in particular.

Ensure that members of the senior management team are familiar with the legislative requirements of the Code of Practice. Particular attention should be paid to admissions, student voice and the ethos that all teaching staff should consider themselves to be teachers of students with learning difficulties/disabilities.

Request that support for students with learning difficulties/disabilities is a regular agenda item for feedback and discussion at management level.

Consider the organisation's admissions policy and consider recommending any alterations required in light of the Code of Practice.

Undertake a review of systems for assessment to ensure that they are designed to identify learners' needs.

Review, or introduce, consequential assessments to ascertain specific needs.

Explore, as appropriate, the organisation of support staff systems in other establishments.

Ensure a good understanding of procedures and timescales required by the Code of Practice.

Chapter 3: Special educational needs in a further education context and the role of the SENCO

Develop an overview of the most commonly occurring learning difficulties/disabilities and what is required to offer support.

Undertake an audit of teaching and support staff to establish levels of awareness, skills and experience of working with young people with a variety of different challenges.

Establish and develop a strong, collaborative working relationship with the relevant colleague(s) in the LA.

Set up an ongoing, non-competitive pattern of liaison with the manager of the discrete provision with the intention of developing skills amongst mainstream staff via in-house training and development (formal and informal).

Establish robust transition strategies for pupils transferring from Year 11 to post-16 departments/centres. This should include links between settings in terms of information, staff and learners.

Chapter 4: Assessment, identification and planning

Review the establishment's assessment policy and assessment strategies. If necessary, develop or acquire additional assessment tools that are accessible to learners with particular challenges.

Undertake an audit among colleagues to assess awareness of indicators of physical and learning difficulties.

Provide training for all staff on the identification of physical and learning difficulties as part of establishment-wide development, e.g. development days, INSET.

Establish whether or not there are organisational colleagues with the necessary qualifications to undertake specific assessments. If appropriate, liaise with other local providers to share expertise.

Ensure that pastoral systems are robust in order that all potential causes for underachievement may be considered.

Audit systems of cyclical review across the organisation.

Publish guidelines for new and existing tutors to establish their responsibility for supporting learners with additional needs.

Survey levels of tutor confidence in the support of learners with learning difficulties/disabilities.

Identify key personnel in the LA and other sectors with whom to liaise to support learners with learning difficulties/disabilities.

Chapter 5: Identifying and managing support needs

In advance of the start of the academic year (during recruitment for new students) undertake an audit of the support needs of all students with learning difficulties/disabilities.

Compare the needs of the students with the skills and experience of existing support staff, including specialisms, to inform any staff recruitment issues.

Having audited learner need and compared this with support staff available, recruit any additional staff, with appropriate specialisms if required.

In advance of the student starting a course, liaise with relevant external specialists to ensure that systems are in place for the learner to access the support needed, with reference to his/her timetable.

Chapter 6: Working with colleagues

Deliver training to the senior management team and governing body on their statutory obligations and also on the implications for practice and resources.

This will not only raise awareness but also keep the issue of support for learners with learning difficulties/disabilities as a priority agenda item.

Encourage members of the governing body and senior management team to attend whole-establishment development sessions (development days/programmes, INSET) on topics relating to the support of learners with learning difficulties/disabilities.

Consider undertaking the NASENCO award qualification, especially if no other relevant qualification is held (see also section 6.5).

Undertake an analysis of staff training needs. This should be done regularly to include new staff and reflect the current cohort of learners.

Develop a programme of training for teaching staff on their role in relation to the support of learners with learning difficulties/disabilities.

This should include generic training to be delivered across the setting, bespoke sessions as required, and information about external and online courses.

Provide or arrange one-to-one training for individual colleagues on aspects of support in which they feel that they are lacking knowledge, experience and confidence.

Ensure that all teaching staff, and TAs, are aware of the descriptors above, encouraging them to seek advice, support or training if necessary.

Ensure that all colleagues with responsibility for arranging work placements take into consideration the needs of the learner (a–c, vii above).

Inform all colleagues, including refectory and administrative staff, of the particular needs or requirements in respect of individual learners with specific challenges.

Work closely with the colleagues responsible for organising staff development opportunities to ensure that appropriate training is available for staff and that this is well publicised, including the facility for 1:1 support if required.

Establish collaborative relationships with external colleagues who support learners with regard to specific challenges.

Ensure that contact between learners and external colleagues is facilitated, while minimising, as far as possible, disruption to a learner's timetable.

Chapter 7: Administration and procedures

Become familiar with the style and format of EHCPs used in the different LAs from which the organisation's learners transfer.

Become familiar with the relevant LAs' evidence requirements and their format.

Obtain the policy/guidelines on 'reasonable adjustments' for the relevant LA.

Undertake an audit of learners' plans/records and other documentation for quality assurance purposes.

Ensure that long-term goals for learners include those, as individually appropriate, that relate to preparation for adulthood, e.g. employment, independent living, community inclusion and maintaining a healthy lifestyle.

Provide training for colleagues to support the setting of meaningful, achievable and realistic targets.

Set up a schedule for each learner with an EHCP, giving deadlines and prompts for the collection of information for reviews.

Ensure that systems for the transfer of information are secure and that they take into account the timescales needed to accommodate the preferred method of delivery for different LAs.

Chapter 8: Working with families, schools and other professionals

Read Annex 1 of the Code of Practice.

At the planning and review stages engage in discussion with learners to establish how they feel about different support methods.

Use best endeavours to establish mutually communicative relationships with families/carers.

Become familiar with the circumstances of families/carers in order to offer a range of different methods of communication and support.

Actively seek additional information from schools or previous providers as required.

Discuss previous support strategies with the learner to establish their feelings about this and the extent to which they found it helpful.

Establish a robust and collaborative relationship with the relevant LA officer/team.

Make contact with other LAs from which learners may attend the setting, ensuring that a relationship is established with a key officer/team.

When setting up and maintaining the schedule for reviews (section 7.5), incorporate the possibility of short timescales. This could be because a review is required immediately or soon after a learner starts the course or due to college holidays when the student is not present.

Draw up a list of the relevant external colleagues involved with each young person, as appropriate, giving contact details, availability and so on, and ensure that communication strategies are in place to maintain effective information exchange.

Where it is necessary for a young person to see an external specialist during college time, facilitate arrangements that will cause minimum disruption to the learner's timetable.

When there is a requirement for a young person to meet an external colleague during the working day, ensure that there is a suitable, stress-free environment in which the meeting can take place.

Chapter 9: Planning for transition

Discuss long-term aspirations and goals with learners either before or at the start of their courses.

Draw up a one-page profile that gives details of aspirations and goals, along with the learner's own views of him/herself and the support he/she needs.

Keep overall goals in mind throughout the monitoring of progress. In order to facilitate this, ongoing feedback from teaching and support colleagues will be required.

If necessary, arrange for the design of bespoke training sessions for learners to assist them with interview techniques, including role play and simulation.

If necessary, arrange for the design of bespoke training sessions for learners to assist them with interview techniques; include role play and simulation within the training.

Ensure that colleagues responsible for advising on/facilitating employment opportunities are fully conversant with the needs of individual learners.

With appropriate colleagues, design strategies to ensure that potential employers are informed and aware of any challenges experienced by learners.

Build up a bank of employers. Include travel considerations, access arrangements and any other details which are relevant to the potential employment of young people with learning difficulties/disabilities.

Engage, at an early stage, in discussions with family/carers and other relevant agencies/professionals to ensure appropriate arrangements are made for smooth transfer into independent/supported living.

Supply relevant information, including support given and progress made, to the new provider.

When placements are suggested or planned, give consideration to any budgetary implications, e.g. support while on placement.

According to the arrangements in place for finding and monitoring work placements, ensure that there is a robust feedback system to inform learners' progress records.

Ensure that support arrangements are put in place, as required, in advance of transition.
Build up a bank of local charities, voluntary organisations and so on, who may be able to support young people in the local community.

References

Blatchford, P., Bassett, P., Brown, P., et al. (2009). *Deployment and Impact of Support Staff in Schools: The Impact of Support Staff in Schools. Results from Strand 2 Wave 2.* DCSF-RR148. London: Institute of Education, University of London.

Burt, C. (1917). *The Distribution and Relations of Educational Abilities.* London: King & Son.

Care Act 2014. London: HMSO.

Cheminais, R. (2015). *Handbook for SENCOs*, London: Sage Publications Ltd.

Children Act 2004. London: HMSO.

Children Act and Families Act 2014. London: HMSO.

Department for Education (2014). *Further Education: Guide to the 0 to 25 SEND Code of Practice.* London, HMSO.

Department for Education/Department of Health (2014; revised 2015). *Special Educational Needs and Disability Code of Practice: 0–25 years. Statutory Guidance for Organisations Who Work With and Support Children and Young People with Special Educational Needs and Disabilities.* London: HMSO.

Disability Discrimination Act 1995. London: HMSO.

Disability Discrimination Act 2005. London: HMSO.

Education (Handicapped Children) Act 1970. London: HMSO.

Education Act 1981. London: HMSO.

Education Act 1993. London: HMSO.

Education Act (Part IV) 1996. London: HMSO.

Education and Inspections Act 2006. London: HMSO.

Education Reform Act 1988. London: HMSO.

Equality Act 2010. London: HMSO.

Feiler, A. (2010). *Engaging 'Hard to Reach' Parents: Teacher–Parent Collaboration to Promote Children's Learning.* Chichester: Wiley-Blackwell

Mental Capacity Act 2005. London: HMSO.

Pickering, S. (2005). *Cognition and Learning Difficulties.* Bristol: University of Bristol

Special Educational Needs (Information) Act 2008. London: HMSO.

Special Educational Needs and Disability Act (SENDA) 2001. London: HMSO.

Warnock, M. (1978). *Report of the Committee of Enquiry into the Education of Handicapped Children and Young People.* London: HMSO.

Sources of further information

British Dyslexia Association
Unit 8 Bracknell Beeches
Old Bracknell Lane
Bracknell,
RG12 7BW
Tel. 0333 405 4555
www.bdadyslexia.org.uk

Equality and Human Rights Commission
Tel: 0808 8005050
www.equalityhumanrights.com

MENCAP
Royal Mencap Society
Head Office
Mencap National Centre
123 Golden Lane
London, EC1Y 0RT
Tel. 0808 808 1113
Help and advice: Tel: 0808 808 1111
www.mencap.org.uk

MIND
15–19 Broadway
Stratford
London, E15 4BD
Tel. 020 8519 2122
www.mind.org.uk

National Association of Special Educational Needs (NASEN)
Nasen House
4/5 Amber Business Village
Amber Close
Amington
Tamworth
Staffordshire
B77 4RP
Tel. 01827 311500
www.nasen.org.uk

National Autistic Society (NAS)
Tel. 0808 800 4104
www.autism.org.uk

SCOPE
6 Market Road
London, N7 9PW
Tel. 0808 800 3333
www.scope.org.uk

Local councils are a source of information regarding local voluntary organisations and charities.

Index

Page numbers in **bold** refer to figures, page numbers in *italic* refer to tables.

Printed in Great Britain
by Amazon

48422524R00070